# WE'RE GOING TO FLY HIGH

Torn Curtain Publishing
Wellington, New Zealand
www.torncurtainpublishing.com

© Copyright 2023 Valmai Redhead. All rights reserved.

ISBN Softcover 978-0-473-69079-3
ISBN EPub 978-0-473-69080-9
ISBN Kindle 978-0-473-69081-6

No portion of this book may be reproduced, stored in a retrieval system or transmitted in any form or by any means—electronic, mechanical, photocopy, recording or otherwise—except for brief quotations in printed reviews or promotion, without prior written permission from the author.

Unless otherwise noted, all scripture is taken from the Holy Bible, New Living Translation, copyright © 1996, 2004, 2015 by Tyndale House Foundation. Used by permission of Tyndale House Publishers, Inc., Carol Stream, Illinois 60188. All rights reserved.

Some names and identifying details of people described in this book have been altered to protect their privacy.

The poem, "What is Life?" is used with permission of the author, Rev Andy Eldred.

Quotes included in the story are taken from personal interviews and are used with the permission of those interviewed.

Photographs are used with permission of the author.

The details in this book are based on the retelling of situations, incidents, and dialogues from personal interviews and external sources, and as such, are not intended as an exact account.

Typeset in Noto Sans, Noto Serif and Fino

Cataloging in Publishing Data
  Title: We're Going to Fly High
  Author: Valmai Redhead
  Subjects: Biography, South Africa, New Zealand, Faith-based biography, Hot air ballooning, Tragedy, Aviation history, Inspirational, Legacy.

A copy of this title is held at the National Library of New Zealand.

# WE'RE GOING TO FLY HIGH

Chrisjan Jordaan's life, love and lasting legacy
and the fatal flight that rocked a nation

### Valmai Redhead

A young couple who died in yesterday's ballooning tragedy had been together for a year after spending time on a church mission to Africa. Alexis Still and her partner Chrisjan Jordaan were among eleven people who died on an early morning hot air balloon ride that went tragically wrong near Carterton yesterday.

**Otago Daily Times 08-01-2012**


A memorial to the eleven lives lost has been unveiled on the fourth anniversary of the Carterton balloon crash. A small crowd gathered yesterday morning near the crash site to mark the tragedy... Power poles that held the lines struck by the balloon stand nearby, looking out over a yellow tree that marks the spot where Alexis Still, 19, and Johannes "Chrisjan" Jordaan, 21, jumped to their deaths. Two small trees planted nearby mark where the balloon went down and nine other lives were lost.

**Fairfax New Zealand Newspaper 08-01-2016**

# CONTENTS

Prologue — 1

| | | |
|---|---|---|
| Chapter 1 | South Africa, 1990 | 5 |
| Chapter 2 | Life is an Adventure | 9 |
| Chapter 3 | Time for School | 11 |
| Chapter 4 | The Dawning of a New Day | 15 |
| Chapter 5 | Destination New Zealand | 21 |
| Chapter 6 | Christjan Meets Sam | 27 |
| Chapter 7 | Family Reunion | 31 |
| Chapter 8 | With Life Comes Change | 35 |
| Chapter 9 | Glendhu Bay | 39 |
| Chapter 10 | Southland Boys' High School | 43 |
| Chapter 11 | Life at the Hostel | 47 |
| Chapter 12 | Rugby and New Mates in Gore | 51 |
| Chapter 13 | A Job, a Car, and an Accident | 55 |
| Chapter 14 | Faith, Famine, and a Scholarship | 59 |
| Chapter 15 | There's No Place Like Home | 63 |
| Chapter 16 | The Emerging God-Factor | 67 |

| Chapter 17 | More than Mates | 71 |
| Chapter 18 | Friends Become our Chosen Family | 75 |
| Chapter 19 | Leadership and Respect | 79 |
| Chapter 20 | Moving On | 83 |
| Chapter 21 | The Tinakori Flats | 89 |
| Chapter 22 | Life Group Evolution | 93 |
| Chapter 23 | Please Send Me to Africa! | 97 |
| Chapter 24 | Attitude Without Words | 101 |
| Chapter 25 | Making a Difference in Malawi | 105 |
| Chapter 26 | Vision and Passion | 109 |
| Chapter 27 | Party Time | 113 |
| Chapter 28 | We're Going to Fly High | 119 |
| Chapter 29 | Back at the Flat | 125 |
| Chapter 30 | Shockwaves of Grief | 131 |

| Commemorations | 143 |
| What is Life? | 147 |
| Gallery | 149 |
| About the Author | 153 |

# PROLOGUE

*Saturday, 7th January, 2012*

Chrisjan did his best to stay quiet as he crept out of bed. His roommate, Melvin, had wished him well the night before and was still fast asleep. Chrisjan was glad. Dawn was still a few hours off, and he didn't want to disturb his friend. Picking up the generous amount of food he had prepared for his special outing with Alexis, Chrisjan headed out towards the car he had borrowed for the day and gently closed the door behind him.

Carterton was more than an hour's drive away, but Chrisjan had left plenty of time to swing past his girlfriend's home before heading out through the Hutt Valley and over the Rimutaka Ranges. For thirty years, Carterton had been a centre of hot air ballooning in New Zealand. Situated close to the capital city, locals and tourists alike flocked to the region, where the micro-climate created perfect conditions for the famous early morning flights.

Chrisjan and Alexis were excited as they pulled into the parking lot at Carterton airport. Check-in time was six o'clock and their pilot, Lance Hopping, was there to meet them. Chrisjan and Alexis gathered with the other passengers, some of them standing with family members and friends. Their sense of eager anticipation was punctuated by introductions and light-hearted conversation.

Lance Hopping had flown hot air balloons for more than twenty years. Today, he explained, they would be flying in a Cameron A-210 model balloon known simply as 'Mr Big.' The passengers looked over to the balloon basket. It was sitting on a tandem trailer hitched to the company's red Toyota. Climbing up beside it, Lance began the morning's safety briefing and explained the launch process. *Keep your hands inside the basket. Don't touch the hoses or gas tanks. In the event of an emergency landing...* Chrisjan and Alexis drew in close to each other as he spoke. With his arm round her waist there was no mistaking they were a couple.

There would be ten passengers on the flight that morning and all of them were keen for a photo opportunity. Alexis' blonde hair was flying wildly to one side, kept only slightly in place by her red beret as she and Chrisjan huddled together in front of the basket and smiled for the camera. It was a winning shot.

With a final wave to their friends and family, the passengers followed the Toyota across the mown grass paddock to the launch site, where they were given the opportunity to assist the pilot and other ground crew in off-loading the wicker basket from the trailer. As always, Chrisjan was right in the middle of the action. Jumping onto the trailer, he helped heave the basket down onto the ground. Next, came the balloon itself. There seemed to be no end to the rainbow-coloured Dacron fabric as company staff pulled and stretched it across the paddock. Next, the attachment cords were sorted and laid out straight. Chrisjan and another passenger,

# PROLOGUE

both wearing safety earmuffs, held the edges taut as a large fan began to inflate the balloon. Nearby, Alexis stood watching, her puffer jacket offering welcome warmth despite the cold air of the fan. By the time the propane gas burners roared to life and the balloon began to take shape, Chrisjan had relaxed into his role and was chatting nonchalantly with the pilot. To anyone looking on he might easily have been mistaken for a staff member.

Finally, the preparation check-list was complete. Lance boarded first and began adjusting the burners as the passengers climbed one by one into the basket. Realising they were the youngest there, Chrisjan and Alexis waited at the end of the queue. Finally, they were all aboard. The rope attaching the basket to one of the support vehicles was released, and with a loud 'whoosh,' the balloon inflated fully and began its ascent into the clear early morning sky.

It didn't take long for the aircraft to reach its thousand-feet altitude. Having waved them off, friends and family below jumped into their cars, eager to follow the flight path in their own vehicles. Others went along in a chaser van supplied by the company. Some forty minutes later, when the balloon had landed, they would all regroup before heading to the Wild Oats local café. Already, the staff that morning were busy preparing a hearty breakfast for their soon-to-arrive guests.

High in the air, the passengers gazed out over vineyards and coastline, mountains and farms. Hot air ballooning is a truly idyllic experience, and that morning's adventure was no exception. Flying conditions were near-perfect, the surreal silence interspersed with quiet chatter and the occasional burst of gas from the balloon's burners. Chrisjan and Alexis relaxed. Too soon it would be time to begin their descent.

## CHAPTER ONE

# SOUTH AFRICA, 1990

Johannes Christoffel Jordaan was born on 4 September 1990. But that is a lot of name to say in one breath, so his father abbreviated it to 'Chrisjan.' The newborn baby was the fifth-generation son to be given the name, and he hoped the shortened version might help avoid confusion within the family. In South Africa, a son's heritage is often embedded in his Christian names.

Chrisjan's early but safe arrival via C-section came as a relief to his family. Weighing just 2.6 kilograms, he spent his first few hours in an incubator so his parents, Annie and Jan (pronounced *Yahn*), were thankful when finally they were able to cradle their healthy baby son in their arms. They had been so worried. Deep sadness at the stillbirth of their first child early in their marriage still lingered. Two healthy children had been born into the family since then, but still the memories troubled them. They couldn't bear to lose another baby. Now, after nine anxious months, their newborn son had arrived, and the family, at last, seemed complete.

From the moment the girls were told that another baby was on its way, six-year-old Anmari took charge of the news. She was convinced this would be a boy, and decided he should be named Charl, after her best friend at pre-school. The day Jan turned up at their preschool to announce to the girls that they really did have a brand-new baby brother, Anmari was so excited she ran through the playground announcing it loudly to everyone, especially to Charl. But it would be five long days before she and her sister, Elrie, could have a cuddle with the new baby. The state hospital's strict regulations at the time insisted that only husbands and children over the age of twelve years were permitted to visit.

This gave the family all the more reason to rejoice on the day that Annie brought the baby home. Three generations gathered to celebrate the long-awaited son. Food was prepared. Relaxed chatter buoyed the mood. Everyone was happy—except Chrisjan, who had not stopped crying since he had received his polio immunisation at the hospital just before being discharged. Throughout the afternoon's celebrations, while the guests happily mingled and chatted, Jan attempted to pacify his upset baby son, determined that not even a crying baby would take away from the joy of the occasion. This newborn was indeed a cherished and welcome addition to their growing family circle.

Six weeks after the birth of Chrisjan, Annie returned to work. Juggling motherhood with teaching at the local school required a delicate balance. Early each morning she bundled her tiny son up and dropped him at the day-care centre, but the arrangement did not last long. Chrisjan was not yet fully weaned when unexpectedly,

## SOUTH AFRICA, 1990

he began to cough. Sitting up in bed with him night after night, Annie soon developed a cough as well. Both mother and baby were diagnosed with pneumonia. Chrisjan, in particular, was desperately ill, and with a forty-two-degree temperature was urgently admitted to hospital. Many difficult and tense days followed. Annie was worried he wouldn't survive. "For the second time, I was afraid we would lose our baby," she said. "That is when I made a promise to God—that if Chrisjan were to live, he would belong to God forever."

Chrisjan pulled through, but just three months later he was admitted to hospital again, this time with gastroenteritis. It was a pattern that would continue through his early years, overshadowing many of the usual baby milestones.

As the children grew, the young family eventually settled into a routine. Life was full, but Sunday afternoons provided an opportunity for Jan and Annie to take a short nap while the children amused themselves. Jan would stick a glass marble onto the door and say, "My eye is going to watch you!" as he turned towards the bedroom.

It was one such Sunday afternoon, while his parents were dozing, that young Chrisjan pulled himself onto his feet and took his first wobbling steps, much to the delight of his older sisters. From that point on, there was no stopping him. Young Chrisjan was all set for a life of adventure.

CHAPTER TWO

# LIFE IS AN ADVENTURE

Adventure was in his blood, but it was also nurtured in Chrisjan at a young age by the stories his mother told him. The traditional African tales of *Tokkelos* and *Snuiter* particularly captured his young imagination. Tokkelos, a short almost goblin-like creature with long, black hair all over his body, was known for his supernatural powers. Superstitious people, afraid of his powers, would sleep with their bed elevated on bricks in case he climbed up to disturb them during the night. But when Annie told the stories, they were not filled with mystical fear. Instead, she turned *Tokkelos* into a naughty dog, and *Snuiter* into a cat who put ideas into *Tokkelos'* head, and along with their antics, she always included a little moral lesson that sparked young Chrisjan's curiosity. "Did they get into trouble?" he would ask his mother. "What kind of trouble?" Annie would smile as she watched her son's mind ticking over with possibilities.

As he grew older, Chrisjan enjoyed real-life adventures too, especially on holiday at their family farm in the north of the country. For many years, Annie and Jan led jamboree-style youth camps, and their three children were always in the mix. Immersed in outdoor life, with plenty of hiking and exhilarating activities to be enjoyed, Chrisjan was never far from the action. Flying through the air one day after being butted by a Damara ram, he landed on the ground some distance away, only to come up smiling. When a snake entered the campsite, Chrisjan was right in the mix as it was being killed. Whether they were visiting the seaside, or undertaking an expedition to the great city of Durban, all of life was an adventure to be enjoyed.

Chrisjan was daring and mischievous, and growing up with two sisters gave him plenty of scope for escapades, fun and pranks. But the South African toddler also had a deep sense of right and wrong. On his first birthday, he eagerly helped Anmari pull up the beans that were just beginning to sprout in his aunt's garden. When a scolding put an end to their fun, the brother and sister made a valiant effort to replant the beans in an attempt to make amends.

Soon, Chrisjan turned two. For this birthday, his mother made him a train-shaped cake, lavishly decorated with colourful, round sweets. When party-time arrived, however, it was discovered that there were hardly any sweets left on the cake. Quick to provide an explanation, Chrisjan announced that they must have disappeared in a puff of locomotive smoke. But when he saw Annie blaming the girls, Chrisjan, ever anxious to do the right thing, owned up and set the record straight. His honesty and protection of others was already emerging as a trait that would shine steadily brighter in the years to come.

CHAPTER THREE

# TIME FOR SCHOOL

The South African schooling system allows students to be enrolled from the age of six, but because of his birth date, Chrisjan was nearly six and a half before he began grade one. Unlike many of the other students, however, he was not the least bit overwhelmed on his first day. After all, when your father is the principal, school seems merely an extension of home. *Rodora Laerskool* was a small school of approximately one hundred and fifty pupils, located in a rural district about a twenty-minute drive from their family home in Randfontein. When Chrisjan started school, his older sisters were already in their senior classes. Soon they would move on to Randfontein Afrikaans Medium (RAM), a much larger school with about nine hundred pupils, where Annie taught.

Not long after Chrisjan started school, the family moved out of town to lease a small rural property. Now they could raise livestock for breeding, an important step towards their long-term goal of full-time farming. At the time, teachers in South Africa could choose to take early retirement and draw down their pension from the age of fifty. Both Jan and Annie were keen to take up that option, and firmly believed that farming would be a most satisfying career to embark on in the future.

The family welcomed the change of lifestyle. Growing racial tension in South Africa's urban areas made it necessary for private homes to have fort-like security, with intruder-proof fences, guard dogs, and the essential alarm system. With their new rural setting came a greater sense of freedom. Of course, they still had to be cautious, and their guard dogs remained a fixture in their new home, but it was a positive move. Now the children could safely go for a walk or a bike ride without their parents. Everything seemed spacious and liberating, from the extra bedrooms in their new home, to the separate family room, and extensive grounds where the children were delighted to discover there was a dam suitable for swimming.

The Jordaan children spent hours making a homemade raft from empty fuel drums, and an aquarium for the frogs they caught. When they tired of the water, there was fun to be had building huts and climbing trees. Chrisjan loved sitting near the top of a tree singing his favourite song, 'I believe I can fly'. Although the cornfields that surrounded the house were out-of-bounds, forbidden territory because they provided the perfect camouflage for insurgents, the girls would occasionally sneak out to explore, and they often conned Chrisjan into joining them. Despite his natural yearning for adventure, Chrisjan tried to be the voice of reason. "We shouldn't really be doing this," he would say half-heartedly, but his sisters usually had little trouble persuading him to participate in the mischief. If they were found out, at least they all would be in trouble together.

The downside to the family's new location was the time it now took for Annie to drive to town. The extra travel time added at least one hour to her working day. For Anmari (and in later years, Elrie), the commute was even longer. For Jan, however, work was much closer—less than a fifteen-minute drive from their new home. Soon, Chrisjan was old enough to attend the middle school, where he met Flippi, Nico, Pieter and Stephan. These boys hit it off from the start and, with their love of rugby, quick wits, and enough mischief to keep the teachers on their toes, they quickly became inseparable companions.

They were happy, fulfilling years. School days began early, before eight in the morning, and with their parents on staff, the Jordaan children got used to amusing themselves while Jan and Annie attended staff meetings or taught extracurricular activities after school. Weekends in the Jordaan household were occupied with church activities and involvement with the Afrikaans youth movement, *Voortrekkers*. This meant that Sunday afternoons were the family's only real downtime.

Like most parents, Jan and Annie focussed on creating a stable home, working hard to make a living, and educating their children. They set goals, planning for the future, and so far, everything seemed to be on track. And yet, despite their move to the countryside, a sense of disquiet was growing. The new millennium found South Africa facing escalating racial tensions and turmoil. Changes in the political climate were happening with alarming speed. Land grabs, squatters, injustice, discrimination and corruption were becoming far too common. The situation was unnerving and the Jordaan family had an ominous foreboding about what was ahead. The African land this family had called home for generations was no longer a peaceful place to live.

Now they faced a harsh reality. Their prospects of farming were rapidly disappearing into a dark, empty void. Their concerns were further increased when the three local schools amalgamated, and Jan's position was swallowed whole as a result. Knowing a line had been marked in the sand, the family faced painful and difficult decisions. It was becoming clear that a better future would mean a radical shift in their life's direction. Together, Jan and Annie weighed the cost. Annie had another year to wait before she could draw down her pension. But for Jan, who was about to turn fifty, there was nothing more to wait for. For him the school bell had tolled for the last time.

CHAPTER FOUR

# THE DAWNING OF A NEW DAY

In the face of South Africa's growing turmoil, any flicker of hope seemed worth pursuing. For Jan, the light filtered through one Saturday morning when he attended an information seminar about emigrating to New Zealand. Suddenly, a country he had never been to captured his imagination, birthing fresh optimism. The possibilities were exciting, even though the logistics of such a move were enormous. Undeterred, Jan threw himself into meticulous research to answer the myriad of questions that accompanied the possibility of emigrating.

At first, Anmari and Elrie did not take their father's enthusiasm seriously. Their wider family also thought he was joking. Everyone expected they would end up farming their family land. Surely this new idea would dissolve as quickly as it had risen! But as the months passed, Jan became more convinced. Together, he and Annie debated the pros and cons of moving to New Zealand, and concluded that it ticked all the boxes. Here was a land where opportunities far outweighed the obstacles. Having made up their minds to 'just do it,' they began to move forward through the labyrinth of documentation and applications.

Their first step was to pack up their home in Holfontein. Regardless of whether they eventually moved to New Zealand, the family no longer needed such a large house. With Anmari now away at university, it made sense to leave their property and return to a more compact home in town. The promise of freedom, security and opportunity in another country held much greater value than the size of a house. Living back in Ranfontein for a time was more convenient and less expensive. Jan's plan was swinging into motion. Taking a temporary position teaching maths at a local high school, he and Annie began preparing for the days ahead. The cost of migration was exorbitant, and every rand they saved would be an investment in their new life.

~

When Jan arrived in New Zealand for a two-week visit he had no idea what would eventuate, but his first impression of Auckland, the country's largest city, was positive. Jan had brought copies of his resumé with him in the hope of securing a teaching job, but it was not to be. One of the strict requirements for immigrant teachers seeking to work in New Zealand was to pass a test in conversational English. With Afrikaans as his first language and Kiwi colloquialisms an enigma to most foreigners, Jan came tantalizingly close to passing, but not close enough. And so, encouraged by his contact person in Auckland, he applied instead for a job on a dairy farm in the South Island of New Zealand. The Southland province could hardly have been further away from his home in South Africa, but with its backbone of agriculture, stunning scenery, and close proximity to tourist destinations like Queenstown, Jan knew it could prove to be an excellent choice.

Jan had not expected to be milking cows on a dairy farm, and there are not too many similarities between being a school principal in South Africa and turning up at a cowshed at five o'clock in the morning, but Jan returned to South Africa with a new perspective on their future life in New Zealand. Sure enough, an email soon arrived to confirm that he had indeed been offered the position. If he accepted, duties would commence just two months later. Having now visited New Zealand, and realising that farming had always been in their long-term plans, Jan was prepared to give it a go. Right away it became clear that saying 'yes' was perhaps the easiest step. Now, there were countless decisions to make, many of them in the next two months. The first decision, was to take only Chrisjan with him.

At that point, the timing was not yet right for the whole family to emigrate. Annie still had work commitments, Anmari needed to return to her university studies in Potchefstroom, and Elrie wanted to focus on finishing her final year at Monument High School. But Annie and Jan thought carefully about the idea of sending Chrisjan with Jan. Having Chrisjan with his father would ease the sense of isolation, and it was a good opportunity to strengthen their father-and-son bond. It would also ease Annie's sole-parent responsibilities. For thirteen-year-old Chrisjan, moving to New Zealand ahead of the family sounded like a bold, exciting adventure. The thought of a long-haul flight and a new life in a different country was more than enough to have him buzzing. But every aspect of his above-average maturity and strong life values would be needed when the two of them headed south-east towards the Antipodes. This was not a mission for the faint-hearted.

For Chrisjan, there was one significant downside to making this journey. Although he was still settling into his first year at Monument High School, he had already made an impression on the rugby field. Rugby was his passion, and he had good reason to be proud of his selection into the B-grade team. Monument High was consistently ranked among the country's top five teams in the South African schools' official rugby rankings. Many Springbok players had been educated there and were held in high esteem as positive role models. Accompanying his father to New Zealand meant that Chrisjan would have to relinquish this impressive opportunity.

He would also be leaving behind his best friends, Flippi, Nico, Pieter and Stephan. There would be no more bike rides together, no more sleepovers at each other's homes, and no more climbing plum trees and pelting unsuspecting passers-by with fruit, or other boyish escapades. There would be no mum around to keep the family on track, and no sisters to annoy or to ask for advice. For six months there would be only phone calls, emails or letters to keep in touch. It would be just him and his dad, and they would need to fend for themselves. It was a big call for both of them.

Leaving his country of birth would not be easy either. With Nelson Mandela at the helm, South Africa in the 1990s was undergoing its own transformative growth as a nation. In years to come, Chrisjan would understand the profound global impact of the apartheid era, the lifting of sanctions, and what it meant for his country to be reinstated at the United Nations Assembly. But while he was growing up, he simply did not see the colour of people's skin. Life was rich and diverse, and Chrisjan learned to show respect to everyone. On one occasion, when Jan took the three children to the African Museum in Johannesburg, despite the many visitors that day, they were the only ones with white skin. Still, they were not fazed, and they never felt threatened. Exposure to a variety of cultures was an important part of growing up in the Jordaan family. When the family went out for a meal, Jan and Annie would often choose to eat at a Greek or Chinese restaurant, rather than simply take the easy option of fast food from McDonald's. New Zealand, in contrast, was far less diverse at the time, especially in Southland.

Chrisjan also knew he would miss the native animals and wildlife which had always fascinated him. Now, their family trips to the nearby Kruger game reserve would be simply a treasured memory. Occasional weekend excursions to a private wildlife ranch owned by their family doctor would be another wonderful recollection. But for now, he would have to be content to push 'pause' on all of those African adventures.

Facing a prolonged separation is not easy for a close-knit family, and this was especially true for the Jordaans. That reality hit them in all its rawness when Annie and the girls, along with three of Jan's sisters, gathered at Johannesburg's O. R. Tambo Airport to farewell the intrepid explorers. There was no going back now. When Jan and Chrisjan checked in with only one bag each, it felt a bit surreal, almost as if they were just heading away on holiday.

Strong family ties, a lifetime of friends and a good reputation don't pack into a suitcase. They knew they would see each other again at Christmas, but that was six months away. Jan and Annie knew their strength and resolve would be tested until they were reunited once more.

~

When Jan and Chrisjan touched down in New Zealand's Queenstown Airport, they were struck by the stark contrast to what they had left behind. Crisp, winter sunshine and blue skies had sent them off. In New Zealand, however, a recent snowfall left the locals freezing, and icy rain pelted the ground, swelling the rivers. Everyone was rugged up in layers of wool, set to face the famous southern cold. But, along with the many other immigrants who were having to rapidly acclimatise to the bracing winds and chill in the air, the Jordaan men soon found themselves donning gumboots and oilskins along with the local farmers.

Jan had known that immigrating to New Zealand would test their strength and resolve. But the severity of the long winter months was only the start. What they could not foresee, was the long 'winter of the soul' that lay ahead.

CHAPTER FIVE

# DESTINATION NEW ZEALAND

Jan and his son were met at the airport by Robert Ross, Jan's new boss. Robert was the sharemilker on a farm owned by Peter Dale. On the two-hour trip south towards Balfour, Jan had opportunity to ask lots of questions. Having come from Randfontein, a metropolis with a population of nearly one hundred and fifty thousand people, the first shock was how small his new town would be. Balfour, where the farm was located, was a township of less than one hundred and fifty people!

Still, the welcome was warm. A little way past Balfour, they turned onto a gravel road before arriving at a small house with three average-sized bedrooms and a cosy living-cum-kitchen area. Jan described it as a Heidi hut, yet they felt grateful for a place to call home. The house was adequately furnished with just the basic necessities: beds, table and chairs, crockery, towels, sheets and a few blankets. Good warm bedding is vital in a Southland winter, but there was barely enough, and Jan and Chrisjan looked forward to receiving more. Annie assumed that South African blankets were the warmest the best and planned to send some out to them and they were very grateful when they finally arrived some weeks later.

Jan and Chrisjan did not have a lot of spare cash. A microwave was beyond their budget, and it was another six months before a washing machine was affordable. Even the hardiest of locals would have felt daunted by the thought of having to wash farm clothes by hand, especially in winter. But Jan had a philosophical attitude, and was determined that he and Chrisjan would get on with making the best of things. They kept the wood burner stoked and dried their clothes in its heat.

More than blankets or appliances, however, Jan needed overalls, wet weather gear and gumboots. A vehicle was another essential. When Peter Dale made the unexpected and generous offer to underwrite the cost of their necessities and said he was happy for Jan to repay him over the following months, Jan was astonished—and relieved! Together, Chrisjan and Jan settled on buying a shiny, red Isuzu Ute. This gave them much-needed independence, and was quite a talking point. Chrisjan phoned Annie, bursting with excitement. "Mum, back home there are all these crap cars, but you have to see this one. It's a fantastic car. It's a cab and a half!" Annie wasn't sure what that meant, but the enthusiasm in his voice was infectious.

The nearest supermarket was in Gore, the main commercial centre for the rural area of eastern Southland. It was about a twenty-five-minute drive, and once a week, they would take their carefully considered list to the New World supermarket. Jan knew their budget was tight, even for groceries, so Chrisjan would keep an eagle-eyed tally, and when they reached their limit he would let Jan know. "We have to stop now. We can't buy any more." The money never went as far as they would have liked.

Neither Chrisjan nor his dad had done much shopping or cooking before. Sometimes, when talking to Annie on the phone, they asked her for recipes. Phone calls were preferable to internet, which was slow and unreliable in their area. They were grateful when Chrisjan learnt new cooking skills during food technology lessons at school. Hamburger patties and blueberry muffins quickly became favourites. Vegetables were easy to prepare, but like many South Africans, for Chrisjan, a meal wasn't a meal without a generous serving of meat. Later, it was supplied from the farm, but at the start, they bought their own. Jan made sure a new pot, big enough to house the chunky, cheap cuts of meat they could afford, was included on the shopping list.

Jan got on well with his boss and quickly learnt the farm routine and settled into work. He was glad to learn that one of the other employees was also from South Africa. But for Chrisjan, one of the biggest changes was going to school. Instead of travelling by car, like many of his classmates, he had to walk three kilometres, then catch the school bus to Northern Southland College in Lumsden, twenty kilometres away. With a college roll of approximately two hundred pupils, the school must have seemed small compared to Monument High where the students numbered twelve hundred, many of whom were friends or family.

His first day was an introductory day for new students, and being quite informal, it gave him the opportunity to find his way around, learn about the timetable, and meet some of his teachers before the rest of the students started. This helped him feel more confident the following morning when it was school as usual and he began to attend classes with other year nine pupils.

Chrisjan reckoned it would be good to have a job during the holidays, and he didn't have to look far. Robert needed someone to grub out the thistles on the farm. Chrisjan was keen, and with no shops nearby, saving his earnings came easily, so it wasn't long before he was able to buy a Play Station. Next, he saved for a pushbike. These became somewhat of a rite of passage as Chrisjan entered his teenage years. Jan could see his son taking responsibility and continue to mature beyond his years. "He learnt very early to think for himself," his father said. "With half the family overseas, it was very difficult. We just had to push through."

Chrisjan took time to adjust. Everything was new, both at school and at home. Each day after school, when he arrived back at their little house, only silence greeted him. There was no family dog barking out a welcome. There were no mates to call. Loneliness fell like dusk, which came by five in the evening during mid-winter. Empty hours ticked by before father and son could share the events of the day. Slowly he got into an afternoon routine of homework, followed by chores—preparing a meal for two, keeping the fire going, and doing dishes. During the first six months, tradition was a significant factor in helping to anchor father and son. On Sunday evenings they would take time to read and reflect on a few verses from the Bible, just as they had always done in their family devotions back at home, and it strengthened the bond between them. Singing a hymn was a bit difficult with just the two of them, but they sang anyway. And very occasionally, on a clear, still night, they would lie on the deck of their little house and gaze at the southern stars. Resilience and perseverance grew because there was no alternative.

It was no easier back in South Africa. As the months passed, Annie faced some tough choices, including selling many of their precious possessions. She faced even more financial hardship during that time than Jan and Chrisjan did. With Anmari to support through university, and Elrie still at home, things were very tight. There was little left, and they lived from pay check to pay check. It was an incredibly hard time, but it made her stronger as a person.

Annie's thoughts were never far from her boys in New Zealand. She knew that in his final year at RAM, Chrisjan had been vice-head boy; he was a popular choice for the role. But she was aware that he would be missing Flippi, Nico, Pieter and Stephan. And yet, she need not have worried. A new friendship was about to unfold in New Zealand.

## CHAPTER SIX

# CHRISTJAN MEETS SAM

*Many will say they are loyal friends, but who can find one who is truly reliable?*

*Proverbs 20:6*

When Chrisjan's teacher introduced him to his Social Studies class, two things grabbed Sam Stevenson's attention. "I remember thinking he was the only one of us that had to full-on shave, let alone touch a razor," and "he was wearing his uniform from his old South African school. It was a blazer, and one of those funny little caps like the caps cricketers wear."

Former Northern Southland College principal, Tom Clarke, also recalled him wearing his South African uniform. "He wore it immaculately, as if he was on the parade ground," he commented. Without a doubt, Chrisjan's striped blue and gold blazer and tie provided a point of difference right from the start. Chrisjan had no way of knowing that the South African tradition of wearing your old school uniform when you changed schools until you could buy a new one, didn't apply in New Zealand. In this rural New Zealand college, it certainly set him apart.

As soon as they could, Jan and Chrisjan headed to the school's second-hand uniform shop to stock up on shorts, shirts, a jersey and regulation socks. This was a popular and affordable option for many families. Chrisjan was not keen on wearing a uniform that was both second-hand and a little too big, even though it made sense because he was a growing teenager. But Jan understood his son's misgivings. Chrisjan felt as if the second-hand clothes labelled him as an immigrant. He'd never had to use the clothes-bank back in South Africa. While to anyone looking on he would have passed for any Kiwi kid, something inside Chrisjan had shifted. He feared rejection but pushed his emotions into a corner and carried on, doing his best to merge into his new school culture.

And, his perseverance paid off. Soon he began making new friends among his classmates but Sam stood out. When he and Chrisjan began talking, they realised how well they got along, and soon developed a steady friendship. It wasn't long before they were having sleepovers and sharing in each other's lives. Over time, that friendship would evolve into a strong bond, one that significantly influenced both of their lives.

~

Sam and Chrisjan's shared love of rugby proved to be a crucial link over the winter months. Chrisjan's fervent passion for the game spilled out, although the contrast with the competitive team selection process at Monument High must have seemed strange.

## CHRISTJAN MEETS SAM

As Sam explained, at Northern Southland College, if you could pick up a rugby ball and run with it, you were on the team. Not only that, but player positions could be changed from week to week, depending on who turned up for the game each Saturday. Chrisjan soon adapted and did not mind whether he played prop, hooker or even a loose forward; as long as he could get those boots on and run on to the field with his team mates, he was happy. Sam's father noticed his growth and maturity on the football field. "I saw that he was shaving already and thought, 'Holy moly, he's goin' to be one of these big six-foot-six South Africans.' I was thinking we need to get him Kiwi-a-tised and get his visas and everything done so he could come and play for New Zealand. But he never ended up getting any bigger."

During the first months, Jan would take Chrisjan to his Saturday games when he could, but when he was rostered for work, Chrisjan had no way of getting there. On those occasions, the team played without Chrisjan. It was a welcome solution when Sam invited him home for the weekend. Travelling together on the school bus on Friday night and returning on Monday morning not only solved the problem of getting to rugby, it gave Chrisjan the chance to be back in a real family for a whole weekend. Although he was shy, he was extremely well mannered and polite. "It took us a while to get him to join in with the family banter," Sam's mum said, but soon, Chrisjan was like one of the family.

Sam's family enjoyed having him around. They soon realised how much he missed his mother and sisters. As Chrisjan grew more confident around them, they began to hear about the little things in life that were not easy. And they heard about the occasional blooper. One morning, Chrisjan arrived late at school, his face unrecognisably swollen. Sam and his classmates wondered who the new boy was. When Chrisjan sat down with Sam, he could hardly believe it was his friend. As it turned out, Chrisjan had pulled one of his hamstrings, so he had been applying Deep Heat to try and take the pain away. He must have wiped it down his legs, then put his hand on his eyes. Chrisjan's comment was, "Thank goodness I didn't put my hands on my private parts!"

Back in the classroom, Chrisjan had to grapple with his teachers speaking English. Back home, he only had one class in English; the rest were in Afrikaans. Adapting to English as his primary language of instruction was a huge adjustment. Learning to sing the national anthem in both English and Te Reo Māori during school assembly must have been a challenge too. But thankfully, not everything was strange. Jan was pleased to discover that New Zealand used an outcomes-based system of education similar to the one South Africa had adopted four years before. He understood how it worked and believed it was to Chrisjan's advantage.

Many other facets of the smaller school suited Chrisjan and it proved to be a positive learning environment. The college values echoed the same values Chrisjan had already grown up with: "Respect for self. Respect for others. Respect for property."

CHAPTER SEVEN

# FAMILY REUNION

By the end of the year, Chrisjan was settling well into the school. There was still no guarantee that life in their new country would work out well, but as winter passed and summer approached, both he and his dad began to feel more at home. They began to look forward to Christmas, when Annie and the girls would join them.

In preparation for their arrival, more beds were required. The grass was growing faster with the warmer days, so they needed a mower. Just before the ladies were set to arrive, Jan bought a washing machine and drier. He hadn't yet earned a credit rating at the big stores so he was grateful he could set up an account to pay off these big-ticket items. And they did not restrict themselves to buying only the essentials. Knowing that sometimes a little thoughtfulness goes a long way, Jan had prepared a surprise. When Annie and the girls arrived, they were delighted to find a decorated Christmas tree waiting.

Annie and Anmari planned to visit for six weeks, while Elrie had come to stay. In the new year, she would attend school with

Chrisjan, repeating her final year of high school. Academic ability was not the issue—she had won a university bursary at Monument High—but she was advised that in preparation for university study in New Zealand it would be an advantage to have a record of New Zealand qualifications. Elrie's future had factored significantly in the family's decision to emigrate. She had been considering a career with the police, ultimately specialising in forensics, but in South Africa progressing in this field would be almost impossible whereas in New Zealand, there were no such barriers.

When the three Jordaan ladies arrived in early December, they expected to find warmth and sunshine. But to Anmari's shock, it wasn't quite as they'd imagined. Having left a beautiful, summer's day in Johannesburg, they flew into Queenstown on a rainy day. In fact, it was the worst summer the region had seen for ten years. The girls had packed summer clothing, never imagining they'd need to take a trip to the Salvation Army's second-hand shop to buy five-dollar clothes. For Annie, the cooler night-time temperatures were especially hard to endure. Getting out of bed at night, her feet felt life they were freezing on the lino floors. It was unheard of in South Africa to light a fire over summer to keep warm, but that was what they had to do. It wasn't until after Anmari and Annie left the country in mid-January that summer truly arrived in Southland that year.

Despite the weather, the Jordaan women received a hearty reception. On the day Annie and the girls first arrived, a small group from the Lumsden-Balfour-Kingston Presbyterian Parish gathered to welcome them with morning tea. Jan and Chrisjan had established a few friendships there, and although they didn't make it to church every Sunday, they had felt supported during their first months by Pastor Trevor Parkinson and his wife, Shirley. Other families from the congregation also offered friendship and hospitality. Ron and Janice Elder came to know them quite well; each week Janice met with Jan to help him improve his English language and pronunciation skills. It was an integral part of him settling into the community. For Chrisjan, conversation had come more easily. Anmari and Elrie were amused to hear their brother speaking with a Southland accent. They noticed Chrisjan rolling his r's like the locals, and his casual *yep* rather than a more formal 'yes' was new to their ears.

The family was happy to be together again, although there was still much readjustment to come. The weekly budget remained tight, but that wasn't the only thing that was stretched. The house that seemed quite small for two was a squeeze for five. The girls had to share a bedroom, with much less space than they were used to. But for Annie, the experience reminded her of holidays on the farm back home. She loved meeting everyone at the church and within the wider community. She made friends quickly during their six-week stay, and looked forward to returning a few months later. Lumsden reminded her of Barberton, where she'd grown up. The flowers, particularly the roses and the arum lilies, enchanted her. But when she saw the nasturtiums, she thought, "if they can grow here, then it is just like home." The home-baking was another childhood reminder—the scones and pikelets (known in South Africa as crumpets) were the sort of good homestyle food she was most familiar with.

For this family there was a lot of catching-up to do. Annie bore the full tirade of Chrisjan's suppressed emotions about his uniform. Just about in tears, he expressed his hatred of the clothes from the uniform shop. Elrie always wore hand-me-downs from Anmari so she was used to that. But being the only boy in family, Chrisjan had never worn anything second-hand. But despite the uniform issue, Annie felt content that everything about the school seemed a good fit and could see God's hand in it all, especially in the fact that the college had a programme to help immigrant children. They hadn't known that when they'd chosen where to send Chrisjan to school—being the nearest school, it was just the obvious choice. But Annie left New Zealand reassured that God had guided them to Lumsden.

In preparation for the new school year, Chrisjan was able to tell Elrie what to expect at school, but for now, it was still holidays and there was farm work to be done. The girls both pitched in, despite the poor weather, and earned a little bit of pocket money to help them celebrate their first Kiwi Christmas. Elrie had her driver's licence, and the Jordaan girls were able to drive Chrisjan over to Sam Stevenson's house near Mossburn. The trip took about forty-five minutes, but it was worth it. After six months, the two boys were becoming best mates.

CHAPTER EIGHT

# WITH LIFE COMES CHANGE

When the 2005 school year began, Elrie fitted in well at Northern Southland College despite being a year older than most of the other girls in her class. Geography was a great subject choice. Field trips to Aoraki Mount Cook—New Zealand's tallest mountain—and to the Hollyford Valley in Fiordland provided a perfect opportunity for her to explore and discover the natural beauty of the south. Proving herself to be one of the school's best hockey players boosted her sense of belonging and achievement. Hockey was not her only sporting interest. Both she and Chrisjan were avid supporters of Super Rugby. They could predict results with uncanny accuracy, especially when their favourite teams, the Blue Bulls, based in Pretoria, and the Crusaders, based in Christchurch, were playing.

~

For Sam, Chrisjan's friendship proved to be an unexpected life-changer. He had endured much bullying in school over the years, and by high school had learnt to keep his head down. He hid from everybody as much as he possibly could, thinking that if he remained unnoticed, he would also remain un-picked-on. But when Chrisjan arrived and they became friends, Sam's problems seemed to fly away. He just became happier and happier with a true friend at his side, much to the relief of Sam's parents, who had been seriously worried. They were acutely aware of the ongoing, negative impact of bullying which had affected him since primary school days. And so, when Chrisjan and Sam hit it off, they were delighted. They recognised that good, strong friends were crucial for their son's future.

From the moment the two boys connected, Lynne and Barry began to notice positive changes. Sam instinctively knew it too. The friends he'd had in the past were the types who dragged others down to make themselves feel better. Chrisjan was nothing like that. Lynne watched Sam begin to grow in confidence. Barry couldn't believe the change either. "It was like turning on a light bulb," he said. "Everybody's got a lot of friends but you can count your mates on your hand; they are the ones who turn up and help you when you are in trouble. And Chrisjan did. If Sam was having a rough patch, he would turn up and have a yarn to him."

The following winter, the Jordaan family was permanently reunited. By now, Sam sometimes came to Chrisjan's house for a sleepover. He was touched by the fact that they made a real effort to speak English while he was staying, and even though the tiny dairy farmer's 'shack' was a squeeze for the family even without a guest, they always made Sam feel welcome. Sam felt as if he knew them quite well already because Chrisjan had talked such a lot about them. Annie was also happy to meet her son's 'other family,' and encouraged the friendship.

School in New Zealand was going well for Chrisjan. By the end of year ten, his school reports included affirming comments: "conscientious, capable, participates fully, homework handed in on time, projects well researched, excellent work ethic, enthusiastic, demands high standards from himself, positive contribution."

The Jordaan family's hope for the future was rising. After eighteen months of upheaval, separation and relocation, they felt their roots were beginning to penetrate a little deeper into the rich soil of their Southland community. Jan had settled well into the seasonal rhythm of farm routines, and he enjoyed a good working relationship with Robert. They were content, and anticipated Jan's position would be long term. But the new year brought the unexpected news that Robert would soon be leaving because of family health issues. This brought Jan's position to an end too.

The upheaval was hard on everyone. Most staff turnover in the dairy industry happens during the winter, so at least Jan had time to deliberate on his next move, and Robert kindly offered to help him find another position. This was an opportunity for Jan to increase his skill base and broaden his experience, with the potential for a more senior role. But with no guarantee he would find a vacancy within the Balfour area, there were other decisions to make. Moving to another district would likely mean Chrisjan changing schools. He was about to begin his eleventh year of school, and the family considered stability during his senior class years to be of utmost importance. They talked to some of Chrisjan's teachers and to other parents, and they searched the internet for options. Once more, their future as a family was uncertain.

Annie began to wonder if boarding school was the answer. As a mum, she felt somewhat reluctant at the thought of him leaving home again as well as shifting schools. A school hostel, with the option of returning home at weekends, would ensure Chrisjan had the best chance of feeling established, confident and connected in the days to come. But that would be expensive, and they were already committed to supporting Elrie, who was about to begin her studies at Canterbury University. Without residency status, she was considered an international student, so her fees were high. Jan quietly reminded Annie, "Remember what we came for. We didn't come for ourselves. It's the children's future. That was our goal. Do what we have to do to give them the best." They both knew they needed to make wise decisions.

When she and Jan sat down to work out a budget, Annie realised she needed to find a permanent job as soon as possible. Every extra dollar earned would help to ensure there were no barriers for their children's future. Annie had been most grateful for some relief work at both Lumsden Primary School and Northern Southland College, and during the school holidays she began working with Anmari, sorting bulbs for the local tulip farm. In the new year they decided to upskill, studying for a certificate in computing and business administration at the Southern Institute of Technology (SIT). From there, Annie found work at the Tall Poppy Books shop in Invercargill.

CHAPTER NINE

# GLENDHU BAY

Every summer Sam and his family went camping at Glendhu Bay. When he asked Chrisjan to join them, Barry and Lynne were delighted that their 'fourth son' was about to discover the great Kiwi outdoor camping experience. For years they had booked the same site for the same two weeks in January. The iconic kiwi campground is nestled on the shores of Lake Wanaka, eleven kilometres past the town hub. If you drove past during the winter, you may not even notice it, but in summer the campground pulses with life, as hundreds of families park caravans, pitch tents, unhook boats, and catch up with friends. In the evenings, the aroma of sizzling steak and sausages mingles with the laughter and tales of the day. It is a place where families have holidayed for generations; grandparents never tiring of telling stories from yesteryear, and how everything is so different but nothing has really changed.

Chrisjan was no stranger to tenting, having gone camping in South Africa with his family. But this summer playground was a little different. He was not used to long, hot summer days. First light would begin to ripple across the water by five o'clock in the morning, and sunset colours would finally fade behind the mountains around ten o'clock at night. There was all day and all night for whatever you wanted to do. Chrisjan could not believe how relaxed Kiwis were. Sam was used to running round in bare feet for hours and coming back to find his shoes exactly where he had left them. Chrisjan was astonished. In South Africa he would not have had that freedom—his shoes would have strayed, rather than stayed in the same place.

Chrisjan had never been on water-skis before, but that summer he was eager to have a go. At first, he was dragged along, almost submerged, behind the boat. Barry would pull up beside him, laughing and ask, "Did you catch any fish while you were under there?" But Chrisjan would not give up until he mastered the sport—he was hooked. Chrisjan was happy to take his turn as the boat boy, or spotter, watching in case the person on the skis fell. The Stevenson's also had a double ski-biscuit, a round inflatable tube towed at speed behind a boat. The boys loved it. Chrisjan and Sam would strap themselves in, and hold on as tight as they could, while Barry would swing them around behind the boat until eventually they'd get flung off. And then they'd strap themselves back in again for another exhilarating run.

If they weren't on the water, the boys were playing camp cricket, a community event enjoyed by many of the kids at the campground. Chrisjan loved cricket, but was certainly more of a batsman than a bowler. If cricket wasn't happening, he might pull out his rugby ball for the boys to kick around.

By the end of each day, everyone had worked up a good appetite. In the best Kiwi tradition, the barbeque would be fired up and a meal prepared. Chrisjan loved the food, especially the meat, and Lynne noticed that he always brought something to share. Once he brought some boerewors, Afrikaans sausages, for them to try. Chrisjan was a huge fan of barbeques. Occasionally Lynne would manage to convince him to eat a salad, but that was the exception, not the norm! He always helped with the dishes, and if there was any meat left on the barbeque from the previous night, he would wolf it down for breakfast.

In the evenings, Chrisjan would sometimes tell his friend stories of South Africa, adventurous tales of daring and danger that his family had experienced. Once in bed, the boys would talk until the early hours of the morning.

Sam loved having Chrisjan there, even for a few days, and as young men, it became a non-negotiable on his summer calendar. "He was never there for the full time," Sam commented. "but he was either there to help us set up or pack up. I think there were a couple of times when he stayed for a whole week. He'd bring food and wine, a beer or two. I guess it was like his Christmas present to us." The boys would have the occasional beer, then go for a walk, their laughter echoing back to the camp behind them. Sometimes they headed into town for a game of paintball or minigolf.

For quite some time Chrisjan continued to call Barry and Lynne, "Mr and Mrs Stevenson." They teased him that unless he called them by their first names, he couldn't come to Glendhu. Eventually he relaxed, dropped the titles, and their relationship felt a little less formal.

Barry was surprised and impressed that Chrisjan was meticulous about shaving every morning, even on holiday. And he wasn't the only one who noticed. A group of girls wolf-whistled at the two boys as they were walking one afternoon. "Is that for us?" Sam whispered to Chrisjan. They continued on their way until they heard the sound again and decided to stop and talk. In the end, one of the girls, Sarah, became Sam's first girlfriend, a fact he attributed to Chrisjan attracting her attention in the first place. Lynne watched the proceedings unfold, amused. She could see that the girls had thought Chrisjan 'quite something.'

Even when Chrisjan later changed schools, his friendship with Sam remained steady. They were best mates both inside and outside of the classroom. All sorts of people gravitated towards Chrisjan, thanks to his genuine, caring nature. He was by no means a fair-weather friend. What he said, he meant. An even greater legacy was played out at Northern Southland College when Sam went on to become head boy. Lynne believes it wouldn't have happened without Chrisjan's influence. For this family, Chrisjan's impact was immeasurable. Lynne didn't hesitate to sum it up, "He brought us back our son."

CHAPTER TEN

# SOUTHLAND BOYS' HIGH SCHOOL

Once the decision had been made, Jan and Annie began the process of enrolling Chrisjan as a boarding student at Southland Boys' High School (SBHS), a well-respected school that drew pupils from all over the province. Although Sam would remain at the college where they had first met, Chrisjan was keen to make the change. He knew he would find some familiar faces, having mingled with a few boys from the school at weekend rugby games. He also knew other boys from Northern Southland College who were also planning to transfer there.

From their first visit, Jan was impressed with the school; one hundred and twenty-five years of tradition echoed through its halls. When they first stepped through the main doors, the first thing they noticed was the Italian marble floor with the school crest crafted into it, filling the foyer. The motto reflected everything they believed: *Non scholae, sed vitae discimus (Not for school, but for life, we are learning)*.

Likewise, the school's core values of compassion, honesty, perseverance, respect, responsibility and service—spelled out in bold, blue lettering across the solid rimu doorway of the hall—resonated with both father and son. And, the All Blacks honours board hanging on the wall inside held twenty-two names of former students. There was no doubt Chrisjan's passion for rugby would be well nurtured.

The school was adapting to changes too. Year seven and eight students had been welcomed for the first time the previous year. This move followed widespread amalgamation of secondary and intermediate schools throughout the country, and increased the school's roll to more than one thousand pupils. The amalgamation was generally considered a great success. As one parent put it:

> "Southland Boys' High School was not just a school; it was a place where boys could be boys, where spirit and character were given a voice, where muscle and brawn were celebrated in positive ways, and where the sound of the haka made the hairs stand up on the back of one's neck."

The new face of the school included a rite-of-passage ceremony for boys progressing from the junior to the senior forms. Chrisjan's orientation also included enrolment at Coldstream Boarding House, across the road from the school. Accommodation for out-of-town students had been an integral part of Southland Boys' High School since 1954. The House Manager, Sue Mills, was struck by Chrisjan's can-do attitude and his smile, which seemed to light up the room.

Most boys were already well established in the hostel, and three of them—Jesse Paenga, Kris Walker and Alex Taylor—became some of Chrisjan's best mates, helping him to settle in and learn the routines. At first the boys assumed that Chrisjan was a 'gap year' student—his 5 o'clock stubble and chest hair made him look like he was in his twenties—but soon enough they realised he was in their classes and their own age. The boys found it hard not to like Chrisjan. He was so full of life, and before long, they felt he'd always been there. They found his stories of growing up in South Africa fascinating—it was nothing like the Southland farming experiences they were all familiar with.

The school didn't have many other overseas students and there were no others in Chrisjan's class, so his arrival helped bring some cultural diversity to the boys' lives. Although he spoke good English, phone calls home were usually in his native Afrikaans. The boys couldn't understand a thing and were quite amazed at how easily Chrisjan switched between the two languages.

Not long after Chrisjan arrived, the conversation one night turned to nicknames. Nearly all the boys had one. Alex was *Digger*, Kris was *Snowy*, and Jesse was *JP*. They tossed around some names for Chrisjan but nothing sounded right—until they began talking about the Springboks, when suddenly someone suggested *Bok*. It stuck, and for the rest of his time at school, everyone knew him by that name.

CHAPTER ELEVEN

# LIFE AT THE HOSTEL

In the hostel, Chrisjan quickly gained a reputation as the king of storytelling. The dormitory rooms at Coldstream were quite typical for a school hostel. Space was adequate but not generous. Each room, divided into bays, housed nine boys. Two beds in each bay were separated by a small bench and cupboard unit. Partitions between the bays did not reach right to the ceiling, so talking after lights-out was easy. There were many long, late-night yarns. Chrisjan loved to keep his new friends enthralled, passing on stories from South Africa of raids, shoot-outs, and poachers who came at night and cut the Achilles tendons of the cattle on neighbouring farms. As he casually recounted each incident, his friends would be left dumbfounded and shocked. These Southland boys, who had grown up within a safe and secure farming background, had never heard anything like it. Yet, he would always finish by telling them "South Africa's a really great place." When they responded "We're never going there!" he would say, "No, no, it's a really great place." No matter what had happened in the past, he really did love his country of birth.

Living in close quarters had its gritty moments. Sometimes Chrisjan's friends would annoy him but he had his ways of deflecting unwanted attention. "Settle down," he would say, poking them in the ribs. His trademark cheeky grin masked his disconcerted feelings.

At times they all pushed the boundaries. One evening, the hostel kitchen door was not locked properly, and for these teenage boys this was an open invitation. Kitchen staff arrived next morning to discover a whole loaf of bread missing. Another night, indoor rugby practice seemed a good idea, and Annie and Jan were sent the bill for Chrisjan's share of the cost of a broken flat-screen TV as well as a few light shades.

Boundaries were pushed in other ways too. Chrisjan's friends realised he could be gullible, and admit that, at times, they probably took advantage of his trusting nature. One of the boys had a ute parked at the hostel with a dog kennel on the back. Jesse asked Chrisjan if he thought he could fit inside it. Once he had clawed his way in, the boys latched the door and ran off to have dinner. When they returned later, Chrisjan was still there, lodged into the dog kennel.

Ever forgiving, Chrisjan wouldn't allow his relationships to be ruined by resentment. He helped his friends with their homework when he could. Although the others would usually bolt quickly when the bell rang, Chrisjan often stayed to continue working. He may not have been a straight-A student, but he was certainly a hard worker. That was what his friends respected him for the most.

Sometimes the boys would invite Chrisjan home to their sheep farms for the weekend. Sheep farming was quite different to dairying, and it gave Chrisjan the chance to help with a new set of chores. It was on his friends' farms that he learned skills like crutching—clipping the wool around the tail of a sheep to help prevent infection. He was always willing to pitch in. His impeccable manners and respect for others never changed. Alex's mum was impressed, saying he was one of the nicest boys she had ever met. Kris' parents said the same. Once, when Chrisjan was staying with Jesse, Annie agreed to pick the boys up after a rugby game on the Saturday. Unknown to Annie, Jesse was staying at his grandmother's home in town that weekend and asked Annie if she could drop him off. Thinking he meant his own home, she was prepared to drive Jesse home and then drive back to Lumsden, a trip of several hours each way. Jesse was struck by how like his mother Chrisjan was. Those values of generosity and courtesy his parents had taught him were deeply ingrained.

CHAPTER TWELVE

# RUGBY AND NEW MATES IN GORE

At first, the boys of Southland Boys' High School thought Chrisjan could well be the next big thing in rugby. When he turned up for the team trials, it was with hopes he would be a loose forward in a number eight jersey. His relatively short stature, however, saw him placed in the front row of the second XV as a hooker. Throughout the season, pulling on the number two jersey fuelled his passion for the game. He didn't miss training. He didn't miss a game. His excellence and dedication inspired all the other boys, including Jesse, who played as a lock. "He'd always spur the boys on if the game wasn't going well. Sometimes he'd go to call the lineout and forget what country he was in and start speaking Afrikaans. We'd stand there waiting for him to call again."

Chrisjan quickly discovered that playing winter sports in Southland was invigorating. He told the boys that back home, rugby games were played in temperatures of thirty to thirty-five degrees. Perhaps the cooler days suited him; by the end of his first season, he was awarded the trophy for the most improved player. Both his ability and team spirit were obvious to the coaches, and on a few occasions, they called on him to play for the first XV. It was a great honour.

Chrisjan was almost as passionate about cricket as he was about rugby. He was good enough to be selected for the school's second XI. School sports day, one of the biggest days on the school calendar, was another highlight, and he participated with raw enthusiasm and energy. Coldstream House was a force to be reckoned with—they had won the shield for twenty-four years in a row. Their house colour was orange, and Chrisjan, Alex, Jesse, Kris and the rest of the hostel boys sprayed themselves from head to toe with orange sheep raddle paint. They were the team to beat and everyone was out to get them. They once walked from the hostel through the quad, only to be charged by the boys from other houses. They ran as fast as they could, then congratulated themselves on being like warriors from *Braveheart*. Every year, Coldstream House won the sports day challenges, and Chrisjan was up there with the best of them. It wasn't until after the friends finished school that the hostel boys were finally beaten.

Later in the year, when other sports were winding down, the boys from the hostel would go out after school and kick a ball around. Some nights they would go over to the school car park and play touch football. It got quite competitive at times. Other evenings would see them playing hostel rugby. It did not matter which side they were on—the boys would just organise themselves into two even teams and rip into it. Even in that informal setting, Chrisjan wouldn't hold back. He saw attitude as important. He might have been 'in it to win it,' but that was never a reason to put anyone down; when he was playing with the younger boys, his positive, inclusive attitude gained their respect.

During his first six months at the hostel, heading home at the weekends meant going back to Balfour. But when Jan found a new job close to Gore and Annie was appointed to a teaching position at Gore High School, the family moved there. Living in a larger town with good amenities was much more convenient for everyone, and it was a welcome bonus for Chrisjan because it reduced his travel time to get home on weekends.

As with every previous move, the family embraced the opportunity to be involved in the community and meet new people. They began to attend the nearby Calvin Community Church where there was a growing, vibrant youth group. Annie encouraged Chrisjan to join so he could make friends outside of school. At first he seemed reluctant. Maybe he thought he had coped with enough changes already. Or perhaps he preferred to not have other commitments when he was spending time at home. School, rugby and travel already filled a lot of his week. But he did go, possibly because he wanted to please his mum, and it was a decision he did not regret; it impacted not only his life, but also the lives of two new friends he met there.

One night, before the evening programme began, the youth were messing around, crashing into walls and narrowly avoiding people, when Chrisjan walked through the doors, his shoulders hunched and his eyes towards the ground. He looked a little uncomfortable, and when a few leaders approached him, he didn't say much. After a while James Bruce, better known as 'Brucie,' went over to talk to him. As soon as they talked about rugby, they had a connection. It was a friendship waiting to happen. James had plenty of mates, but had been really wanting a close Christian friend who was the same age and had prayed that God would send someone into his life. The night Chrisjan arrived, Brucie's prayer was answered. Later, Brucie recalled that moment Chrisjan arrived at the church. "He walked through the doors and I thought, 'Thank you, God. He's going to be my friend.'"

Sam Johnstone was also a member of the youth group, and although he was a little younger, he too had a passion for rugby. When the youth group attended local youth festivals, they would always take a rugby ball. If the three boys weren't play-fighting, there was a good chance they were playing touch rugby. As time went on, Sam looked up to both Chrisjan and Brucie as strong role models.

Chrisjan did not attend youth group every week to begin with, so it took time to truly connect with the other boys, but over the following years, his involvement with the youth group became a non-negotiable, and their friendship lifted to another level.

CHAPTER THIRTEEN

# A JOB, A CAR, AND AN ACCIDENT

When Chrisjan turned sixteen, he got serious about saving for his future and towards the end of the year, a job vacancy advertised in the local paper caught his attention. Mark and Wendy Brocket needed help in the milking shed on their dairy farm near Kelso with extra hours available during school holiday. When Chrisjan turned up for his interview, he introduced himself simply as 'Chris.' The Brockets could see he was keen, had a good attitude and seemed 'switched on,' and the hands-on experience he had gained with his dad at Balfour was an added bonus. There would be little overlap of the busy season on the farm with his winter rugby commitments, so it was a perfect fit and they hired him. During peak season, with about six hundred cows, each round of milking could take two people up to four and a half hours and would mean traveling forty five minutes from home, long before dawn every weekend. Few of his peers would have been keen to take on such a commitment. But Chrisjan, who had grown up in a family with a strong work ethic, was not daunted.

At first, he was dependent on his family for transport but, realising he needed his own vehicle, Chrisjan began saving. Over the Christmas holidays, unbeknown to his parents, he bought a car for nine hundred dollars. But his pleasure was short lived when an oil leak and a failed suspension quickly rendered the car useless. Chrisjan cut his losses and sold it for parts, but it would take many more months of saving before he could afford to buy a reliable car of his own. For the time being, he was back to borrowing a family vehicle or depending on his family to drive him to work.

One morning, Chrisjan was driving his father's red Isuzu home from work. This was a privilege he exercised with all due diligence and care. He was a good driver and was careful on the road. But about half way home, he was momentarily distracted and lost control. The vehicle swerved, snapped a concrete power pole in half on impact, then careered through a fence and rolled into a paddock. Barry and Janine Harvey, who lived on the property, heard the commotion. Pulling on her shoes, Janine rushed outside and was relieved to find that Chrisjan did not appear to have sustained any injuries. But she could see he was in shock and took him back to the house. When Chrisjan phoned his parents, he was very worried that they would be upset. When they arrived, they were simply thankful he was not seriously injured. The police were called and the vehicle was written off, but there were no serious consequences.

For sixteen-year-old Chrisjan, however, the accident was a defining moment that magnified the God-factor in his life. Realising how much worse the outcome could have been, issues of spirituality and faith began to take on new importance for him over the following months. Friday night youth group was another catalyst for that change. Back in South Africa, in the church where he had grown up, Chrisjan's faith journey would have been quite different. There, the gatherings had been more formal, with hymns and liturgies a regular part of their weekly services. When they first came to New Zealand, it had taken the family some time to adapt to the more relaxed worship style often accompanied by drums and guitars. But by now, the youth group had become an important part of Chrisjan's life. So adjust, they did.

CHAPTER FOURTEEN

# FAITH, FAMINE, AND A SCHOLARSHIP

Chrisjan's second year at Southland Boys' High School was busy from the start. His new role as a dormitory leader at Coldstream brought extra responsibilities, but there were benefits too, including a more spacious, semi-private sleeping area, separated by a curtain from the main dormitory. He was well suited to the role, and the dorm boys respected him. Because Kiwi culture was different from what he'd grown up with, Chrisjan had to adjust his expectations. Back home in South Africa, a younger boy would always hold a door open for a senior student, but that did not happen in New Zealand. If any younger ones did give him a bit of lip, he would simply sit down and have a 'yarn' with them. The strategy seemed to work.

He was keen to connect with other Christian students. He found them at *Powerhouse*, a group that met weekly during lunch hour. He also was given permission to attend *Primal*, a youth church which met one evening mid-week in the city. The other boys soon realised this was part of who he was and occasionally they asked a few questions. Kris noticed he always had his Bible beside his bed and read it every night.

Jesse discovered that Chrisjan wasn't the sort of person who would try to push his faith onto others. "If you were interested," he remarked, "Chrisjan would cheerfully sit down and tell you more, but if you weren't, he was happy just to leave it. He wouldn't force it on you."

Alex was amazed at how much Chrisjan knew about his faith. He recalls, "Some nights we used to sit in the dorm and all talk; you'd ask and he would just come out with all this stuff and he'd just roll on. It was quite mind-blowing."

Whenever there was opportunity to put his faith into practice, Chrisjan was keen. In previous years, the Powerhouse group had spearheaded a fundraising initiative within the school to support World Vision's annual 40 Hour Famine. Often it had seemed hard to rouse enthusiasm, but Chrisjan was motivated and keen to be involved in the challenge. That year, Grant Meyer, a Powerhouse staff member, was very happy to let him take a lead. He remembers him as a boy who was "charismatic, an extrovert who participated with enthusiasm and who shared his Christian beliefs without compromise."

Sure enough, Chrisjan gathered a few supporters, promoted the event at school assembly and encouraged class participation. In an effort to bring a visible focus he opted to grow a beard for forty days rather than fast from food. The boys were expected to be clean-shaven at school, but the hostel manager agreed to make an exception to the rule for this worthwhile cause, and soon other boys joined Chrisjan and the fundraising gained momentum. The total they raised that year exceeded that of any previous years.

Impressed, Grant Meyer decided to recommend Chrisjan for the World Vision Senior Scholarship week. Applicants were required to have shown leadership, creativity and initiative in their local fundraising efforts. Chrisjan certainly fulfilled the criteria and was chosen as one of thirty pupils from around the country. He was thrilled to discover that his new friend from youth group, James Bruce, was going too.

Their trip to Wellington later in the year included a tour of the Beehive, New Zealand's parliament buildings. Meeting other students from around the country and sharing ideas during interactive sessions helped them to gain an understanding of what it means to be an advocate for change. Exploring concepts that required lateral thinking and interactive leadership development challenged and expanded their worldviews. During that week, they met key social leaders including members of parliament, university lecturers and World Vision staff, each of whom brought a different perspective. The students returned home with a better understanding of world poverty, together with a greater awareness of the goals of World Vision.

The experience was significant for Chrisjan in other ways too. He was struck by Wellington's architecture, noticeably different from the rest of New Zealand. This planted a seed for his future study choices.

The following April, Chrisjan and his mum took a three-week trip back to South Africa. The days were crammed full with adventure. They spent time in Cape Town and at the farm where Jan's ancestors had first landed and settled. The Jordaan family were French Huguenots who had established themselves as winemakers. As well as exploring some of their family heritage, one highlight was visiting the Echo Caves. These massive spectacular limestone formations had been a tourist attraction since 1959. Parts of the caves are dangerous, and there are restrictions as to who can go in. Chrisjan loved every moment of the adventure, and discovered quite a different perspective of South Africa.

Annie was there to attend to some business matters, but the highlight for Chrisjan was meeting up again with his friends, Flippi, Stephan, Pieter and Nico. Fun was never far away when the boys got together, and after a sleepover at Nico's house, they went to school together the next day. This provided the perfect opportunity for a bit of mischief. Everybody in the class remembered Chrisjan because it was only three years since he had left. But the teacher didn't know who he was. Nico told her, "Miss, you have to speak English. He is from New Zealand and he doesn't speak Afrikaans at all." The teacher began to teach and translate all that she said. The boys burst out laughing because they had fooled the poor lady. Fortunately, she didn't hold it against them.

CHAPTER FIFTEEN

# THERE'S NO PLACE LIKE HOME

Home had come to mean many things to Chrisjan. After a year of living in Gore, the family moved once again. Jan had found a much more suitable job in western Southland, with a three-bedroom house included in the package. Meanwhile, Annie was delighted to be offered a full-time position teaching at Heriot primary school with an adjacent school-house provided. This was the break she needed to work towards completing the process for her New Zealand teacher registration.

And so, the family was united in purpose but separated by the available job opportunities. Most weekends Chrisjan headed to Annie's home. Driving from Invercargill on Friday nights, he would go to youth group in Gore, then drive about forty minutes to his mum's house. From there it was only a short distance to the Brockets' farm where he worked on weekends. Occasionally Chrisjan was able to go and stay with his dad, who grabbed any possible opportunity to watch him play rugby. There was a lot of travel involved, but it worked and kept them all connected.

Sometimes on a Sunday evening, Chrisjan and Annie would drive two hours to spend time with Jan, only just making it back to the hostel in Invercargill before the ten o'clock curfew. By the time Annie arrived home, midnight had all but tolled. Despite the change in their family's living arrangements, Chrisjan remained settled and focussed on his studies, and somehow fitted in extra-curricular activities. Every day of the week buzzed with action.

The end of term three was not far away, but at the hostel everything else paled into insignificance as the 2007 Rugby World Cup approached. Excitement was high as the pool games got underway but, in the end, it turned into the year that most Kiwis want to forget. The All Blacks suffered a humiliating quarter-final loss to the host country, France, while the Springboks turned in a winning performance and took the Webb Ellis cup home. On the morning of the final, Chrisjan's friends were sitting watching the game on the hostel's television room. It wasn't until after the game ended that Chrisjan walked in, beaming. "See that footy?" he asked gleefully. The boys were livid! In that moment, they didn't want to know their South African friend.

Towards the end of his second year at the hostel, Chrisjan arrived one Monday morning driving a purple Ford Laser. After his experience of buying a dud car, he had been more careful with this purchase. Although his work at the Brockets' had given him a healthy bank balance, he didn't quite have the funds to buy the car outright, so his mum had agreed to be his guarantor for the extra finance needed. It was his ticket to independence.

Jesse, Kris and Alex were in the dining room when Chrisjan came in with a big grin and pointed out the window. The boys were less than impressed with his choice of colour, make and model, but Chrisjan was as proud as punch. Later he bought a stereo system and enlisted their help to install it. They decided it was time for a bit of fun. A small whistle from the two-dollar shop, wired up and tucked into the exhaust was all that was needed. When Chrisjan started the car, the loud whistling sound startled him. He promptly turned off the ignition and tried again. The same thing happened. He revved the engine. It got worse. He thought his car was wrecked, until they came clean and he realised it was a practical joke.

Their opinion might have bruised his self-esteem, but the purple Ford Laser became a big part of Chrisjan's life. It was economical and reliable. Still, he had to budget carefully. He had made a commitment of forty dollars a month to sponsor a child in Tanzania with World Vision. There was a trade-off; buying snacks and treats at the local shop after school was pretty much off the table. But for Chrisjan, it was a small sacrifice to make. The car gave him his freedom for both school and work.

By the time Chrisjan began his second season with the Brockets they had installed cup removers in the milking shed, and with this updated technology they were confident he could handle the whole process on his own. Chrisjan was up for the challenge. During school holidays they always had plenty of other jobs as well. Working for twelve or thirteen hours a day was never a problem. Before calving began, Chrisjan helped Mark clean out the old woolshed ready to be used as calf pens for the new season. Moving a truck and trailer load of sawdust by wheelbarrow took a while but he and Mark would race each other to finish the task. Mark knew Chrisjan enjoyed jobs that involved vehicles. His eyes would light up as soon as Mark told him to take the bike on an errand. He would hoon up the driveway flat-tack. He loved driving the John Deere tractor too.

Chrisjan made it a point to always arrive at work on time, even if it meant a little sleep deprivation. Mark and Wendy enjoyed the natural, relaxed way in which he related to their family. He always joined them for meals and sometimes he stayed overnight. Wendy noticed how well he connected with their children, playing with them and buying them presents at Christmas. For Chrisjan, it was almost like being part of another home and family.

CHAPTER SIXTEEN

# THE EMERGING GOD-FACTOR

*Don't let the excitement of youth cause
you to forget your Creator.*
*Ecclesiastes 12:1*

*Get Smart*, a youth conference held in several main centres across New Zealand at the time, was always a highlight of the July holidays. Hundreds of young people from around the country were seemingly propelled towards the event as if by an invisible force. For the kids from Gore, fundraising to attend was as much part of the adventure as the eight-hour road trip to Christchurch. As the 2007 conference approached, one of the girls kept badgering Chrisjan, telling him he should go. Her persistence paid off and he signed up. He had never been to anything like it before. It would prove to be a life-changer.

The conference lasted for four days with live bands, techno lights, and a mosh pit where the teenagers flocked to worship. When the music faded and the lights dimmed, speakers from all over New Zealand and beyond delivered powerful, topical addresses, helping a new generation discover God in a way that was relevant to them in the twenty-first century. They couldn't get enough.

Outwardly, Chrisjan's life seemed on track. But that week, radical change occurred on the inside. This was more than an emotional spike—he had a powerful, personal encounter with the Holy Spirit. It was as if his well-learned and consistently practised Christian values jumped out of the rule book and took on an X-factor, triggering a passion and desire to live a God-honouring life, a life of commitment, purity and wholeness.

Jase Barron, a youth intern at Calvin Community Church, noticed the transformation in Chrisjan. After the conference, he seemed to have come out of his shell and was ready to be more open with people, more genuine. Jase saw what took place in Chrisjan as both a conversion and a confirmation. Chrisjan had known all the faith-facts, thanks to his solid Christian upbringing, but now it had clicked that God was relevant to him too, and he owned it.

James Bruce also noticed the change in Chrisjan. From that point, their friendship moved to a deeper level. Now they had more to talk about than rugby or school; there were life issues to be unpacked. Chrisjan also began connecting with others in the youth group more freely, seeking to befriend some who were on the outside edge of the group.

The boys at Coldstream noticed something else. Chrisjan stopped swearing. These country kids used a few well-chosen expletives from time to time without even thinking about it. They guessed he wasn't allowed to swear at home, but at the hostel it probably helped him to fit in with everyone else. They thought it was strange when he stopped, but no one thought to ask him why. They just assumed he had decided to change. But back at Calvin Community Church, when Chrisjan shared during a Sunday morning service what had happened in his life, he pulled no punches. He told it like it was, even about the swearing.

The following year, Chrisjan attended Get Smart again despite an unfortunate clash of dates. During those holidays he could have represented the school, playing for the First XV rugby team. It amazed James and Jase that he passed up such an opportunity. They were almost in awe of their mate who would give more priority to a Christian event than to rugby. It showed exactly how much sport-mad Chrisjan had changed. His priorities and allegiance had shifted and nothing was going to stop him.

Youth Pastor, Marty Redhead, identified him as one of the key senior leaders in the youth group. He had seen a reserved young man now emerging as a 'committed' and 'on fire' man of God. Chrisjan was well respected by his peer group, and he also helped to lead the younger kids who met at an earlier time for their youth programme. And so, to nurture Chrisjan's leadership potential further, Marty offered him the opportunity to attend a Christian leadership course. The commitment involved traveling to attend the course one evening a week for eight weeks, but Chrisjan didn't mind. He was keen for any chance to develop quality character skills and saw it as a worthwhile investment of his time. The purpose of the course was to 'provide nurturing guidance for young people with potential and passion for leadership.' Those words were uncannily predictive of the qualities that would continue to shine out of his life.

CHAPTER SEVENTEEN

# MORE THAN MATES

*As iron sharpens iron, so a friend sharpens a friend.*
*Proverbs 27:17*

As Chrisjan continued to display character attributes, his friends were amazed. James, in particular, could not believe his level of commitment. His work ethic was excellent. Not only did he study hard for school and work on the farm, but Chrisjan would also mow his mum's lawns, attend youth group, help Jase with set-up and leading the younger ones, not to mention his rugby. And somehow, he still managed to give everything his best effort. James would tease him and call him crazy. Sometimes he would text him: *"Bro, come hang out."* And Chrisjan would text back, *"Have got to work today, I'm helping out with . . ."* James would feel respect and exasperation at the same time. But despite his schedule, their relationship was important to Chrisjan, and he would occasionally turn up after work or on his way to a rugby game. Quality over quantity seemed to be his friendship motto.

Jase appreciated Chrisjan's help at youth group, especially during his final year of school. In fact, he saw Chrisjan as his right-hand man. No matter the task, Chrisjan would be happy to help out, and would often ask what could be done. No matter what else he had on, he was ready to get involved and lend a hand. Often, that would mean him staying at youth group until ten or eleven o'clock at night, before heading home in order to be ready to begin work at five the next morning.

Those times of being Jase's right-hand man were never more evident than on Exo Day, a one-day festival hosted by Calvin Youth for senior high school kids to 'chill out' after their end-of-year exams. The event took over the whole church complex, including the car park, and for extra room they borrowed the playing field of the high school next door to run zoned activities like paintball, car-smash, art, crane swing, digger and auto fun.

Inside the building, the team set up zones for PlayStation alongside a girl's pamper zone, op shop, bookshop and café. Bands pulsed out live music until it was time for food, a full roast dinner, no less. Any excess energy could be worked off during evening worship before settling to listen to a speaker. The event drew hundreds of local kids. Chrisjan was in his element and took on specific responsibilities. Some of his friends from Southland Boys' High School supported him; Kris offered a couple of old paddock cars which had been used to race around the farm. He and Jason made the sixty kilometre trip from Gore to Winton to pick up one of the cars on a trailer. After dropping it off they went back and got the other one. On the day, kids just broke them up with sledgehammers.

Kris was glad to help out his friend. No one could doubt Chrisjan's commitment to the cause!

Despite his ridiculously full schedule, Chrisjan managed to find time for recreation. After a decent snowfall, he, Sam and James decided to drive up to the Blue Mountains. Between them, they had one snowboard. The three of them hiked to a peak, Sam in the snowboarding boots, the other two in gumboots. Sam, of course, flew down on the board while Chrisjan and James tackled each other, rolling down in the snow. They were soaking and cold, but had wild fun. When they finally reached the bottom, they headed back to James' house, where they climbed into a go-kart they had built and raced it through the puddles. If they hadn't been soaked already, they were now!

Still, of all the activities in Chrisjan's life, rugby still gave him the most enjoyment, especially when Gore High School, where James attended, played against Southland Boys' High School. The boys found great amusement in grinning at each other across the bottom of the ruck. They started jabbing one another, "Hey buddy!", chortling at their own joke. Chrisjan's friendships were so strong that they could even withstand being enemies on the rugby field!

CHAPTER EIGHTEEN

# FRIENDS BECOME OUR CHOSEN FAMILY

For James, having Chrisjan in his life was almost like having another brother; he already had three so one more didn't make a lot of difference. His parents, Colin and Lynette, didn't mind either—their home was always open, as was their holiday house at Lake Manapouri where James and Chrisjan went to study for their seventh form examinations. The lake, just across the road, was an inviting distraction. James, who knew he could easily give in to the temptation to play more and study less, credited his exam success to Chrisjan's influence. "Probably the only reason I passed my physics papers was because of his integrity and work ethic. When he said he would do something, he did it. In the morning we would study until about twelve o'clock; we helped each other. Then we went and played in the afternoon."

The boys wanted to go out on the lake in the Bruce family's boat, but they had a problem. Chrisjan's car had no tow-bar, so clearly some Kiwi ingenuity was needed. There was a hook on the back of the car, designed for securing a tie-down or rope. The boys found a bolt and attached the drawbar of the boat trailer through the hook. It worked somewhat, and they took great care, but the trailer still dragged on the ground all the way to the boat ramp. Thankfully it was only a short distance, as it made a terrible graunching sound. Now all that was needed was to slide the boat into the water and power their way across the lake.

Chrisjan went to Manapouri more than once with the Bruce family. Sam Johnstone and other friends would often go too. Summer daylight hours were long and the boys had no trouble filling the time with water sports, hanging out, or using up energy jumping off the holiday house roof. In a particularly memorable adventure, a group of boys went to the Grebe River where they put Chrisjan on a riverboard—a specialised bodyboard with edges, designed to help the rider catch eddies and give more control. The rest of them were in the kayaks. They found it hilarious, watching Chrisjan fly down the river, smashing into rocks as he went. He would just bounce off the rocks and keep going, seemingly unfazed, the kayakers paddling alongside. James asked him, "Are you alright, bro?" He just replied, "Yeah, yeah." Chrisjan was clearly out of his comfort zone, but he loved the adrenaline rush.

James Bruce recalls the day. "I remember we went into an eddy—like recirculating water where you are reasonably safe—and it was kind of flushing at the bottom and there was actually a tree at the bottom of it, which is kind of dangerous because you don't want to get stuck in a tree. But Chrisjan floated into it. I pulled the board out and he was hugging the tree. I had to yank him over the tree. The water was pretty slow-moving at that point because he was in the eddy but still, it's not a good place to be. It was pretty exciting. He went home and told his mum all about it but told her not to worry because James was a trained lifesaver. That shows you how worried *he* was."

All the boys greatly respected Chrisjan's example of hard work and sense of adventure, but Sam was particularly struck by his generosity. Chrisjan's car was his prized possession, but when Sam, who had just got his learner's licence, asked if he could have a drive, Chrisjan responded "Yeah, yeah. Get in mate." Sam, wanting to look cool in front of their other friends, went around the first corner too fast and slid, nearly crashing the vehicle. Chrisjan's first reaction was, "Oh no! You've spilt my drink." He didn't seem to care at all about his car. He did notice, however, that Sam was a bit shaken up. "I'll just drive us off the gravel and onto the tarseal," he said. But once they got to the sealed road, he said, "Jump back in, mate," and Sam drove all the way to Gore from there. Another time, Chrisjan gifted Sam his workout machine. Sam had asked if he could use it, and Chrisjan replied, "You can have it if you like." It would have been worth quite a bit of money, but Chrisjan was not fussed about material possessions. He never expected anything in return.

Sam also looked up to Chrisjan for his stance on drinking. "Being involved with rugby, there is this classic drinking culture; it is a huge thing in Southland," Sam explained. "Chrisjan was really into it, but then he decided it wasn't for him and he just stopped. He told all his mates down there in Invercargill he had stopped. I could just imagine the way he would have said it . . . he wouldn't have been judging them."

The boys at Southland Boys' High School accepted Chrisjan's uncompromising stand on alcohol. Jesse remembers that on one occasion he sober-drove for them until about five o'clock in the morning. They didn't know that he had to go to work. He dropped them off before heading out to Heriot, more than an hour's drive away. Kris summed it up: "Drinking wasn't his thing but he never said anything about us doing it. He'd always hang out with us. He was always there."

CHAPTER NINETEEN

# LEADERSHIP AND RESPECT

*A person with good sense is respected.*
                              *Proverbs 13:15*

In his final year at Southland Boys' High School, Chrisjan was named as a prefect. His friends at school didn't know he had been selected until his name was called at assembly; he hadn't thought it necessary to tell them. He wore his badge with pride and honour and willingly embraced his duties and responsibilities, including mentoring younger pupils and contributing to committees for organising sporting and social events. Prefects organised the school ball. Community involvement, such as selling poppies for Anzac Day, was also expected.

The Anzac Day commemoration service at Southland Boys' High School is a most poignant and sombre ceremonial occasion, recalling the fated mission to Gallipoli and the massive loss of ANZAC (Australia and New Zealand Army Corps) lives. Honours boards hang on the wall beside the stage, filled with more than a hundred names of former pupils who sacrificed their lives during the two world wars. Each year during the school memorial service, about twenty-five of the men are remembered. One by one, school prefects read a short vignette of each man and place a poppy beside his name. It takes five or six successive years to recognise all the past students who died as servicemen. The poppies remain in place until the following year. Like his fellow prefects, Chrisjan placed a poppy beside a name, recalling with respect yet another young man whose full potential was never realised.

Alan Bailey, the assistant principal at the time, recalls, "Chrisjan was a boy who showed old-fashioned respect to his elders. He had a strong moral code, exhibited excellent behaviour and attitudes together with good sporting and academic combinations. He was always eager to assist and help. Once he got something in his mind he really worked hard and would strive to achieve his goal. He was very goal-oriented. If I had a school full of him, I would be out of a job. His character made him a good choice for a school prefect."

Chrisjan knew good grades mattered. Over the course of three years at Southland Boys' High School, his achievements reflected his diligence. He received various prizes for graphics, general excellence, English and physical education. In his final year, he was awarded the graphics prize. It was his best subject. His graphics teacher said, "Over twenty-five years I have probably taught something like three thousand students. There are probably ten I would remember and one of those would be Chrisjan. He was outstanding, salt of the earth, one hundred percent polite."

## LEADERSHIP AND RESPECT

Towards the end of 2007, Chrisjan packed up his belongings at Coldstream and headed home to Annie in Heriot. Like all senior students he was beginning study leave in preparation for sitting his final exams. When his exams began, he moved to live with his sister Anmari who was renting a house at Seaward Downs, a small rural area thirty minutes' drive out of the city. She was studying for a teaching degree but her flatmate had married and she was on her own. It was an ideal arrangement and he never returned to the hostel.

Although work commitments separated Annie and Jan, they were very happy that at least Anmari and Chrisjan could enjoy a sense of family life. Their brother-sister bond was as strong and resolute as it had been growing up back in South Africa. Everything was up for discussion between the two of them, even personal matters. Once, Chrisjan confided in Anmari that he felt embarrassed because other boys noticed his hairy chest. He persuaded her to give him a wax treatment but it was far more painful than he had bargained on, and he never asked for another one. Although Anmari was busy with her own studies, she always had a listening ear for Chrisjan. She noticed he spent a lot of time at youth group and recognised the value of the good friends he had made there.

As his final school year drew to a close, Mark and Wendy offered Chrisjan a position as a full-time permanent employee on a new property they had purchased, and he was tempted to accept. However, his parents were not keen. Jan firmly believed that it was important for his son to experience other options in life besides farming. He wanted him to make wise choices in the future and knew that tertiary study would help him gain a wider perspective. Given his natural aptitude for graphic design, pursuing architecture as a career seemed a natural progression and a logical choice. Getting accepted into the School of Architecture at Victoria University in Wellington was a tough process, so when confirmation of his acceptance came, he was elated.

The time had come for Chrisjan to step out through the big, ivy covered portals of Southland Boys' High School for the very last time. He already had his copy of the school magazine *Southlandian*. Each year it includes a pithy, tongue-in-cheek profile of the prefects compiled by the Head Boy. In 2008, it was Michael Carroll who had the opportunity to sum up Chrisjan.

> **Chrisjan Jordaan**
> Nickname: Bok
> Probable destination: World Vision
> Trademark: Accent, beard
> Favourite saying: "Settle down"
> Hero: Mother Teresa
> Favourite pastime: Third year veteran of second XV
> Love to watch: Michael Carroll
> Claim to fame: Being South African

Chrisjan took his profile all in good fun. Now, while many of his peers turned their sights towards University in Otago or Canterbury in New Zealand's South Island, he looked forward to moving to Wellington.

CHAPTER TWENTY

# MOVING ON

Emerging into the wider world once school days have ended is a major transition for both teenagers and parents. A supportive community makes it a little easier to cope as the pages of life turn and a new chapter beckons. Apart from his family, Chrisjan's friends at Calvin Church were his closest community. His final youth event was the Leavers' Service in February 2009, an informal evening where Chrisjan shared his dreams, plans and goals along with others who, like him, were on the starting blocks, poised and ready to launch into careers or tertiary education. Those who had already made the transition in past years shared with warmth and honesty both their highlights as well as their best-forgotten moments. Wisdom in life cannot be learned merely from books.

Saying goodbye is never easy, but finally the sorting, packing, planning, high-fives, hugs, and "see-ya-later" moments were done, and the day came when Chrisjan left Southland to head north. Annie took a week off school to travel with him. In Christchurch they stayed in a backpackers' hostel overnight. The next morning,

Chrisjan delivered his purple car to Elrie who was still studying at university. He had no further need of it and she would find it useful. He and his mum then continued in Annie's car to the Picton ferry. In Wellington they booked into a hotel for one night before Chrisjan moved into his student accommodation. That evening, pausing in the labyrinth of life, they took time to reflect on this important rite of passage. Their family custom of reading a few Bible verses and praying together was simple and meaningful. Then came the moment when, for the first time, Annie shared with him the vow she had made to God all those years earlier. "I promised God that you would belong to Him forever," she told him.

Chrisjan's new home was a room at uStay, a block of inner-city apartments designated as student accommodation. Jono, a Resident Assistant (RA) there, was responsible for looking after first-year students, though he and Chrisjan first met when they were playing touch down on Oriental Parade. Chrisjan was wearing a blue Bulls jersey, showing support for 'his' team in South Africa. Jono found him a funny guy and a keen sportsman, but didn't at first realise he was also a Christian.

Jono attended ARISE Church in Wellington, and had organised a beach party for uStay students to meet other Christians. Chrisjan was keen to attend Sunday services with Jono but was cautious about becoming overcommitted. When he eventually went along, he discovered hundreds of people pouring through the doors of the Michael Fowler Centre, where the church met to worship. Many were students, most were under forty years of age, but there were people of all occupations and ages, all mixing and mingling with ease. Chrisjan enjoyed the contemporary Pentecostal-style services with vibrant music followed by relevant, dynamic, Bible-based preaching, but he felt pulled in two directions. The first year of studies was vitally important; competition was tough, and only those with the highest grades were selected to continue. Completing assignments at weekends helped him to meet deadlines, yet church was important for him too.

Then one weekend when Jase came up from Gore to touch base, he, Chrisjan and another friend all went to ARISE together. That friend began a journey with God that day, and wanted to discover more, so Chrisjan kept attending each week to encourage him. Soon he began to get more involved. He made time to go to Jono's mid-week student life group and their friendship began to grow. Arthur Tse, another leader who went on to become a Care Pastor, noticed that Chrisjan appeared to be a little shy and unsure at first, but gradually grew in confidence. When the life group got too large for one place, Jono established a new group. Chrisjan joined him there, and introduced others into the mix.

By the end of his first year in Wellington, Chrisjan was happy and settled. He was making new friends and had taken on a few responsibilities at ARISE. He had managed to find a balance between church and study commitments, and when final exam results were posted, he was elated with his marks. His parents would be proud that he had qualified for a place as a second-year architecture student. It was the natural progression, and one his family and friends expected him to follow. Instead Chrisjan found himself grappling with a decision he had not anticipated—he was considering taking a gap year to complete a twelve-month internship at ARISE. This would mean stepping outside his comfort zone, but it was an opportunity which captured his heart and challenged his faith.

In one direction lay a career in architecture and a creditable future already being shaped with confidence, skill and ability. In the other direction, signing up to complete an internship felt like a magnetic pull in his spirit that was hard to resist. Chrisjan knew he had to make a choice. He had worked with diligence to reach this point and did not want to make an unwise decision. He also knew that taking a gap year was possible. He discussed his dilemma with Jono and talked to Jase in Gore, who had just completed his second year as youth intern at Calvin Church. Both affirmed his thoughts. But Chrisjan had no idea how his parents would respond. They had given up so much for their children's future, and he didn't want to dishonour their sacrifice in any way. On the other hand, he wanted to honour God and make his life count. Finally, with much trepidation, he phoned home.

His mum answered but on hearing the news did not know what to say. She felt shocked and upset at what Chrisjan wanted to do, and was worried about telling Jan. As it turned out, Jan seemed less worried than either she or Chrisjan had imagined. He took a pragmatic view, thinking a gap year would give Chrisjan an opportunity to think through and experience other options after a year of study. And so, when Chrisjan left uStay at the end of the year, he also closed his architectural study books and enrolled as a church intern.

That Christmas, Chrisjan went home and once again worked at Brockets' farm over the holidays. After a short holiday at Glendhu with Sam and his family, he returned to Wellington, ready to begin the internship programme. Completing a level four Certificate in Christian Ministry was part of the internship requirements, and for his practical work, Chrisjan chose to work with young adults. At the time, this group was known as HUGE, and their key themes were: community, mission, and encounter. Chrisjan worked with a small group of young men, and meeting them for life group and other social activities became the highlights of his week. He also helped organise and lead the annual young adults camp and conference, and had many opportunities to assist the pastors and church leaders. To help support himself throughout his internship, Chrisjan took a weekend job as a night porter at the luxury, boutique Bolton Hotel where he always went above and beyond what was expected of him.

CHAPTER TWENTY-ONE

# THE TINAKORI FLATS

The next change in Chrisjan's life was a transition to flatting. Jono, together with another friend, Cam, had discovered a 'really flash place' in Tinakori Road. They didn't expect to find a flat there. Wealthy and distinguished residents had once walked this street, none more famous than author Katherine Mansfield. These days, galleries and boutiques create a unique neighbourhood ambience for discerning buyers. Cafes and restaurants line the pavements. Neat houses, many of them two-storied, cluster together as though protecting the secrets and gossip of their affluent past.

For Jono and his friends, even more exciting than the illustrious history, was realising that Premier House, the Prime Minister's Wellington residence, was just down the road, hidden discreetly behind a dense screen of trees and locked security gates—unlike the flat at number 271 which did not have so much as a picket fence to separate it from the world. The front door was clearly visible, about five steps in a straight line from the footpath. Like the street, the house had a colourful past.

Jono and Cam went to visit the flat together. It had two stories, with six big bedrooms. It used to be a brothel so there were locks on all the doors. But when the boys found out that the forty-two-inch television came as part of the flat, the deal was done. It only got better when they went around the back and found a basketball hoop!

Several times, one of the flatmates noticed the Prime Minister at the time, John Key, driving past—once with Hillary Clinton, and once with the Warner Brothers. They felt like they were in the centre of New Zealand's political landscape. But soon enough, Tinakori Road became home. The flat quickly became a hub for students and workers from ARISE.

Chrisjan was the only Southlander among the group, but his new flatmates, Jono, Vicky, Lucy, Cam and Israel held him in high regard. He was both genuine and encouraging, which they appreciated and valued. His strong faith and reliability made him a stalwart in the flat environment. Ranon, another flatmate who joined in remembers, "When Jono first brought Chrisjan to church I saw this short, really hairy guy. I thought he was twenty-six or something, and I asked, 'What sort of job do you have?' He replied 'No, I'm studying; I just started this year.' He was like a Southern man who stuck out in stubbies ... *especially* with the stubbies."

For Chrisjan, wearing practical, hardwearing stubbie shorts as a student helped him feel comfortable and relaxed. Back in rural Southland it was commonplace to wear them, both on the farm and when you drove your Ute into town to collect a few messages.

Chrisjan soon came up with nicknames for everyone. Vicky was *V.V.*, Jamiee was *JuJu*, Ranon was *Indian*, Adam was *Adamus*, Lucy was *Lulu*, Israel was *Izzy*, Jono was either *Asian, Muffin or Monkey* because when Melvyn moved in he was also affectionately dubbed *Asian*. The flatmates decided Chrisjan also needed a nickname: *Christofelton* or *C.J.* were favourites.

Chrisjan roomed with Cam, and later, with Melvyn. It was a small room for two, with only enough space for one desk, but it was never a problem. They made it work. Chrisjan was an early riser, getting up around six o'clock in the morning to read his Bible and pray in the lounge. Sometimes the flatmates would hear him singing quietly. Life at the flat settled into a rhythm for everyone. Studies, assignments and work commitments were squeezed between life group, parties, movies, or dinner with friends. Couch space was in demand because there was always someone needing to stay over. At some point, Alexis Still, a local Wellingtonian who also attended ARISE, began regularly visiting the flat to catch up with her friends, Lucy, Jaimee and Vicky.

When it came to food and cooking, Chrisjan had his own ways of doing things. He hated onions and what he called, "weird Asian food." Meat was essential. If a meal didn't have meat he would ask, "Where's the substance?" If there were any leftovers, he would devour them. If he cooked rice, he always had gravy to go with it. Gravy was his favourite. Once he saw Lucy tipping out some leftover gravy. He was incensed and interrupted, "Hey! What are you doing?" And on one occasion when he was cooking meatballs for Alexis and accidentally spilled the juices for the gravy, he almost cried.

When he wasn't in the kitchen, or studying, or at church, or having coffee with a friend, he enjoyed watching movies. His list of favourites included *Modern Family, Law Abiding Citizen, Remember the Titans, Coach Carter, The O.C., Band of Brothers, Braveheart* and *What Happens in Vegas*. Of all the Disney movies, *The Lion King* was at the top of his list, especially once he began dating Alexis. They often joked about their two favourite characters Simba and Nala, almost as if they were playing out their own roles in the Lion King story.

CHAPTER TWENTY-TWO

# LIFE GROUP EVOLUTION

At the flat, Jono and Chrisjan teamed up to lead another life group, but it came with challenges. Several of the boys who turned up were struggling with drug and alcohol addictions or a sense of hopelessness in life, but Chrisjan and Jono weren't fazed. They organised hangouts and barbeques to help the boys connect. For Simon Chu *(aka Simo)* especially, the group was life changing. He had not grown up with a church and had no idea what one looked like.

It was the barbeques with free food that enticed him, and he was friends with Ranon, not even realising he was a Christian. Ranon made a deliberate effort not to sound 'holier-than-thou,' and so when Ranon mentioned that his new place had a basketball hoop out the back and hosted regular meals, Simon decided to drop round. When he arrived, he was welcomed by the sight of someone standing at the barbeque flipping chicken nibbles while holding a torch in his mouth. The guy cooking was Chrisjan, and he made Simon feel right at home. It was a very typical picture of who he was.

The word got round about the meals and hangout opportunities, and soon the numbers grew. Simon became a regular. "I came for friends but I stayed for Jesus," he later said.

Life group was not just a one-night-a-week commitment for Chrisjan. Between meetings he would keep in touch with 'his boys' via text. Often, they wouldn't respond, but he never gave up. One of the young men, Nate, discovered just how patient Chrisjan could be. Chrisjan invited him over for lunch and he gave an evasive, "Yeah, I will" answer. Chrisjan was calling him regularly, trying to set up a time, and Nate would refuse to answer, unable to understand why on earth he wouldn't just take the hint and give up.

Eventually, Chrisjan got hold of Nate's best friend, Jordan, to invite him to the young adults' camp. Jordan was happy to agree. They went on chatting and when Chrisjan realised he was at Nate's house, he asked Jordan to put a reluctant Nate on the phone. "Hey man, I haven't talked to you in ages," was his understated opening. The reality was, he'd avoided Chrisjan's calls for months. Chrisjan invited him along to camp too, and after an awkwardly long silence Nate finally agreed. "Cool, man," Chrisjan replied, then added, "Hey, if you can't afford to come, I'll pay for you."

That was what struck Nate more than anything. He had been ignoring Chrisjan for the longest time, and he was still willing to give to him. Later he said, "Because of that moment, because of that seed Chrisjan sowed in my life, my life changed completely and I've never turned back. That was such an amazing lesson and such a testament to the great man that he became. He continued to see the good in people, and never gave up."

There are many more such stories. Joe grew up in church but hadn't been attending regularly since he'd started at university. After a friend invited him to ARISE, he met Chrisjan, who sent him texts often enough to keep in touch, but not so often that he felt hassled. But when Joe began going to their life group, he never looked back. Chrisjan's humble, welcoming attitude and the nicknames he gave everyone at the door, were part of what made their group so special. Joe's nicknames included *Joe-easy* and *Joe-Joe*, which was eventually upgraded to *G.I.* No one who came left feeling unseen.

By the second year at the flat, the life group numbers had multiplied. With twenty-four guys, it was too many for one group so they divided into two. Jono led one, while Chrisjan, Simo and Nate began leading the other. If Nate ever felt annoyed when people didn't text him back or answer his calls, he remembered Chrisjan's patience with him. Chrisjan had set an example of tenacity and perseverance; he refused to give up on people and kept on pursuing because he believed each one had a purpose for their life.

Although Chrisjan's life was jam-packed with studies, work and church responsibilities, he always made time for family. In the April holidays, he took a break and joined his mum and Elrie for a few days' holiday in the upper North Island. Four months later he went on another trip, this time with a very different purpose.

CHAPTER TWENTY-THREE

# PLEASE SEND ME TO AFRICA!

*Outstanding people have one thing in common: an absolute sense of mission.*

Zig Ziglar

From its inception, ARISE church has supported mission in many forms, both locally and globally. Sharing the love of Jesus in a practical way is an important part of ARISE culture. As well as engaging in initiatives like breakfast clubs in schools, 'Big Hearts' boxes at Christmas, providing disaster relief, and offering support for prisoners, refugees and solo mums, ARISE had recently commenced a partnership with World Vision. Their humanitarian mission of 'working with children, families and communities to overcome poverty and injustice' aligned with the ARISE global vision to serve others.

Chrisjan liked the fact that the church set aside donations for World Vision and provided opportunities every year for members to get hands-on experience overseas. Many church members sponsored World Vision children. Chrisjan already sponsored five-year-old Sumayi from Tanzania, but now his attention was drawn to an upcoming project in Malawi. Chrisjan was quick to put his name on the list to be part of the ARISE team who would travel there. Alexis, did not hesitate either. Finally, she would be able to meet Precious, her sponsor child!

Raising four thousand dollars each was a big goal, but everyone was motivated and keen. Chrisjan's work at the Bolton Hotel helped. But there was still a shortfall, so his flatmate, Israel, who was a site supervisor with a building firm, mentioned an opportunity to work as a labourer on a large upcoming job. The work involved digging a huge amount of dirt out from under a house, and the boss was glad to give Chrisjan a try. Once a week, he'd come down and give it his all for the day, and was paid minimum wage for his efforts. Israel's boss was impressed by Chrisjan's diligence and respected why he was doing it too.

Chrisjan relished the opportunity to visit countries close to his heart and was eager to help facilitate the plans. Pastor Brent Cameron was the team leader for the Africa trip, supported by Linda Cousins, an ARISE intern in Christchurch who worked closely with Chrisjan to facilitate the itinerary. The remaining team members were from Wellington. A couple of weeks before leaving, Brent and Linda flew up from Christchurch to meet the rest of the team. As it turned out, of the ten people on the team, four, including Chrisjan, had an African heritage.

There was a lot to be packed into their fortnight-long trip. First, they were to visit a village in Mozambique where a fellow ARISE member, Anna, and her African husband, Felito, were working. Practical help was needed there for some building projects. Their second week would be spent in Malawi as guests of World Vision. There they would visit the Chata Development Project, which had recently been completed, and then the Lipiri Development Project, which was just getting underway.

The team flew out of Wellington at four o'clock in the morning. It was mid-August, and Chrisjan had just come off a night shift at the Bolton. It was at the airport that Alexis first introduced Chrisjan to her parents. Chrisjan and Alexis did not know each other very well at that stage, but her parents were keen to meet a team leader, and Chrisjan was one of the interns responsible for the team until they reached Sydney. Alexis was just eighteen years old, and naturally they were concerned for her well-being. Chrisjan couldn't answer all of their questions but he did his best to reassure them. After arriving in Sydney, everyone was pleased to meet up with Linda and Brent before flying on to Johannesburg and staying overnight with Linda's brother, who lived there.

The next day, they drove to Mozambique via the Kruger National Park. For Chrisjan and Justin, another teammate who had been there before, this was a highlight. Chrisjan acted as an unofficial tour guide, sharing his love of the natural world in which he had grown up. A tour through Kruger is an experience that cannot be rushed. Impalas, giraffes, a herd of elephants and a rhino have all the time in the world. For the Kiwis, it was a once-in-a-lifetime experience. As Chrisjan and Justin shared their knowledge and passion for the wild, rugged outdoors—what they both saw as the pure side of life—with the other team members, a deeper friendship bond was forged between the two of them.

Throughout the two weeks in Africa, Chrisjan and Justin took every opportunity to introduce their friends to other childhood memories. Dried meat delicacies like *biltong* were a favourite. Every time they saw a shop, they would rush in and buy varieties made from different animal meats—springbok, buffalo and kudu. They loved sharing it all with their New Zealand teammates.

Closing time at Kruger was six o'clock at night. The team was reluctant to leave but knew they still had a couple of hours driving ahead of them before they reached the border of Mozambique. Officials there were strict, intimidating and slow, and by the time they arrived at their destination, it was very late. Setting up camp outside the village in total darkness was almost mission-impossible, especially when they discovered that their borrowed tents had mismatched flies, pegs and poles, but the Kiwi 'can-do' attitude prevailed and with perseverance they managed to create a haphazard combination that worked.

Chrisjan and Justin worked hard to help sort the gear and did not complain that their tent was one of the smallest. They soon devised a workable strategy of squeezing in and lying diagonally to sleep. This was camping at its most basic level. They had utensils and food but that was about all. They didn't even have a gas cooker.

CHAPTER TWENTY-FOUR

# ATTITUDE WITHOUT WORDS

When Justin asked Chrisjan why he had wanted to go back to Africa, his response was that he wanted to love people differently from the way he had when he lived there. In South Africa, it was very easy to get caught up in the political turmoil. For Chrisjan, leaving as a thirteen-year-old, he had been too young to have experienced it himself, but he was very much aware of what went on. Returning to Africa, he wanted to love everybody and help wherever he could, rather than seek revenge. Africa as he remembered it was still there, but he was ready to go back and view it with a fresh, positive outlook; to act out of pure intentions. Justin was challenged and encouraged by Chrisjan's attitude.

Susan, another member of the team, didn't know Chrisjan very well but during their time away she too noticed that he was always thinking of others. Before Pastor Brent woke up each morning, Chrisjan would get up to make coffee for him. With no electricity supply, this was not quite as simple as turning on the electric kettle. First, he needed to light a fire, then 'put the billy on to boil.' For Susan, it was an example of what it meant to show honour. "He taught all of us to honour our pastor," she said, "It was always in him to lead, not with words, but with service. If you needed anything, he didn't tell you, he showed you. He was just so humble. The whole time he would carry your bags, get you water . . . you name it. For me personally, I thought if that is what an internship does to someone's character, I want to be an intern."

While the team was in the village in Mozambique where Anna and Felito's ministry was based, they all worked hard, but not without incident! One day when Chrisjan was gathering branches to build up a wall around the toilet area, he noticed the distinctive creepy feeling of bugs on his skin. Unbeknownst to him, one of the branches was covered in fire ants—large, bright red insects with a bite like a bee-sting. All of a sudden, Chrisjan began leaping around, waving his arms and yelling as he tried to shake them off. A group of village ladies sitting under a tree started laughing at his antics, but Chrisjan was not a happy camper. Every time the team went back to the area, Chrisjan warned them that fire ants happened to be attracted to that kind of tree sap.

The team helped build a church in the village, constructing the walls and ceiling from *kinesu*, or thin bamboo. It was a half-hour drive from the village to the source of the building material. The mode of transport was a three-metre-long flat-deck truck, but with no straps or covers available and loading regulations non-existent, Chrisjan and Justin were responsible for keeping the load on board. Standing a thick bamboo stick in each of the corners of the truck deck, they then loaded the kinesu higher than the top of the truck's cab. In order to hold it down, Chrisjan and Justin lay on top while the truck travelled along the highway. Every time the vehicle stopped, the top layer of kinesu would slide forward, then slide back again when the truck started moving. They felt almost as if they were going to slide right over the top of the truck, but they worked out a rhythm, stayed safe and enjoyed the fun.

While the boys were busy building the church, the girls fostered positive relationships with the women in the village—talking, helping with village chores and playing with the children. Everyone noticed that Alexis seemed to have a natural affinity with the children who loved the funny songs she would sing, and imitated her as they followed her around. In the evenings, the team would gather with the villagers to share about Jesus through music and testimony.

On their final day, the new church building was dedicated and the village celebrated with an African party. Goat stew was on the menu but unfortunately, Justin and Alexis took ill a few hours later. Vomiting and diarrhoea is never pleasant and is even worse on a road trip. Not knowing if the cause was food poisoning or a gastro bug, the team commenced the three-day trip back to Johannesburg and then flew to Malawi where both of them were promptly taken to the nearest hospital to be checked by doctors. Part-way through the consultation, one of the team members realised it was a gynaecological hospital, which generated some light-hearted banter. However, their symptoms were concerning and when someone wondered if it was malaria, the team, led by

Chrisjan, gathered to pray. There was much thankfulness and relief when Alexis and Justin recovered sufficiently to continue on with their travels.

CHAPTER TWENTY-FIVE

# MAKING A DIFFERENCE IN MALAWI

Malawi is a small country nestled between Zambia, Tanzania, and Mozambique. Known as the 'warm heart of Africa,' it is also one of the least developed countries of the world. It is just one of many countries where World Vision has implemented programmes to help address the needs of the people.

When the team arrived, customs officials quickly singled out Alexis to search her luggage. Any tall, attractive blonde girl would have stood out, but being familiar with both the language and culture, Linda was quick to intervene. Without hesitation she said to the officer: "You want to do her suitcase, you do all our suitcases." Then she beckoned to the other girls, "Come everybody, put your suitcases up here." The officials dropped their guard and waved everyone through without any further delay. Finally, they were on their way to the Chata Development Programme.

Seth Le Leu, then World Vision Director for International Development, hosted their visit. The timing was perfect. The local people were ready to celebrate. After fifteen years, their goal had been achieved. Now they were equipped and resourced for a sustainable, profitable future. World Vision had met and engaged with the local people to build trust and find the best way forward. From there, hope had been built through fresh opportunities and skill training. In the Chata programme, one hundred and ten teachers had been trained, one hundred and seventy farmers were established in agricultural cropping programmes, and a further fifty farmers had been helped with establishing backyard gardens. But now the local people were ready to take over the responsibility for operating and sustaining their projects. This handover of full ownership gave everyone a reason to celebrate. The ARISE team members felt honoured to be guests at the graduation ceremony and even to present medals to those involved.

With such a special moment fresh in their minds, the team moved on to the Lipiri Development Programme, where World Vision was about to commence stage one. This was the project the ARISE church in Wellington had committed to supporting. The groundwork of building trust with the local people was underway. Practical ideas were being discussed and considered. Like communities everywhere, the people simply wanted a sustainable future.

A highlight for the Wellington team was meeting children they had sponsored. World Vision staff gathered them together at a local school and as each child's name was called, they stepped forward, and their sponsor (or team member standing in for the sponsor) presented them with a named gift. Smiling and laughing, the children grinned for photos. Alexis was thrilled to meet her child, Precious. Chrisjan's child, Sumayi, lived in Tanzania so he did not get to meet him, but meeting the children in Lipiri was still a highlight for him.

By the time the team left, they had gained a unique understanding of the difference World Vision development programmes make in a community. They had seen the Lipiri programme being established, and they had witnessed the success of the Chata programme. It enlarged their understanding and insight and would help them share the vision with the church back home.

Towards the end of the trip, team members began to notice a new friendship developing between Chrisjan and Alexis. Their personalities complimented one another. They each seemed to have a natural gift for connecting with the local people. The idea of returning at a later time appealed to them both. Rather than being an end in itself, the trip marked the beginning of new possibilities.

CHAPTER TWENTY-SIX

# VISION AND PASSION

*Every man dies, not every man really lives.*
*William Wallace, Braveheart*

Chrisjan celebrated his twentieth birthday on the day the mission team flew back into Wellington. The experience had changed him, enlarged his vision for the future and led him to make two important decisions. The first was to return to full-time study. He wanted to equip himself with skills that would be useful to help people living in third-world countries.

Deciding to train as a nurse was a momentous step. It was a U-turn that no one expected. He had been brought up within the traditionally conservative Afrikaner culture where nursing was regarded as the domain of women. Real men became farmers or took up a profession; very few would consider a career in nursing. But Chrisjan told his friend James that he wanted to serve the people in Africa. "My heart is for them," he said. Training as a nurse was part of fulfilling that passion.

The other decision he made was to date Alexis Still, only there was one small problem: Alexis was on a self-imposed 'boy fast'. Plenty of young men had shown an interest in her, but she figured she had a lot of living to do and most of that happened in the fast lane. She was never without friends, but she felt that a boyfriend would take up too much time. This made it easy to say no to dating. There was another reason too; she wanted to connect with God without distraction, to discover His purposes for her life.

The 'boy fast' finally came to an end though, and not soon enough for Chrisjan. When he formally paid a visit to ask her parents if he could date her, they were impressed. The other girls in the flat became Chrisjan's unofficial advisors. They knew she was cautious about relationships with boys and he was happy to consult them on all things feminine.

The two of them would certainly see a lot of each other because Alexis had also enrolled in a nursing studies programme at Massey University. Their first semester papers included biology and chemistry. Neither of them had planned to study sciences so they had some catching up to do. Later, Alexis picked up psychology as well as cross-cultural communication and media studies. Her passion for people in third-world countries did not stop with nursing. She wanted to study journalism as well so that she could write about her experiences and inspire others.

Despite their full-time study, Chrisjan and Alexis never wavered in their commitment to the church. Chrisjan was responsible for leading one of the sound and lighting pack-in teams, which meant getting up at four-thirty on a Sunday morning once a month. The team would meet at five o'clock in the morning at one of several central-city lock-ups where the gear was stored, load it into a truck owned by the church, and take it across to the Michael Fowler Centre for the day. It was a small truck, so more than one trip was needed. Rigging speakers, hanging lights, setting up video production, placing screens and running cables all had to be done, and when the set-up was finished, musicians and vocalists needed to practise. Working to a tight schedule meant teamwork was essential if everything was to be completed before people began arriving for church at ten o'clock.

Thankfully, in the evenings, packing down was a lot faster. Because church began at five in the evening, the team could begin dismantling the gear around seven-thirty and have the job done and dusted by around ten-thirty at night. Later, he took responsibility for a second team, which meant going through the routine every two weeks. Not many people would be so committed. To further equip himself for a potential return to Africa, he continued with weekend work as a builder's labourer. By the time the second year at the flat was underway, the hours of each day overflowed with activity.

Alexis was involved with children's programmes and drama productions at church. Just as in Malawi, the Kiwi children loved her. It was not unusual for her to be spotted in a huddle of children, still entertaining them after their class had ended. They never wanted to leave. Activities and study certainly did not stop Alexis from making time for friends, or from regularly inviting them to her home. She loved celebrations, often making cupcakes for people's birthdays, family times, and lunch or dinner dates. Somehow, despite their busy year, Chrisjan and Alexis still managed to spend time together. She had many reasons to visit the flat in Tinakori Road because she always liked to catch up with her girlfriends who lived there.

Chrisjan loved the modern, vibrant, creative culture in Wellington, yet until now he had remained unchanged by the 'glitter and glamour' of New Zealand's capital city. But dating Alexis Still soon changed his life and before long, his stubbies were left in the drawer, replaced by skinny jeans, the kind he had said he would never wear. He bought a waistcoat too and even began using hair products. As his twenty-first birthday party approached, Chrisjan would have easily passed for a city boy.

## CHAPTER TWENTY-SEVEN

# PARTY TIME

*Carpe diem – Seize the moment*
*Horace (Roman poet)*

September was the month none of the flatmates would forget. Chrisjan's twenty-first birthday was on the fourth, and a few days later the first of the 2011 Rugby World Cup games would kick off. Both events called for a party.

Chrisjan was planning a low-key celebration. Annie had discussed it with him on the phone and expected to visit. When he told his mum that he was simply planning a day of paintball with friends followed by a barbeque, Annie began to think she might be in the way so she changed her mind and stayed at home. Elrie had decided to go, so at least the family would be represented. In fact, it was Alexis who helped Chrisjan plan the party, which soon evolved into something bigger than he expected. By this time, the two of them were a couple who were clearly in love.

On the night of the party, when it was time for speeches, Jono insisted that Chrisjan and Alexis sit together on the couch. Anecdotes about the two of them were woven into nearly every speech, making it seem almost like an engagement party. But it really was Chrisjan's night, celebrating another significant rite of passage. It was special to have Elrie there to meet his friends and hear the stories and the laughter.

Plentiful food was a priority that night. Chrisjan would never have a party without meat. The beef and pork roasts were a bit overcooked, but it didn't seem to matter. Coleslaw provided a simple but perfect side salad. He didn't want anyone to go hungry so he bought one hundred and sixty bread rolls as well, but most were left untouched. Four months later when they were packing up the flat, they found them, stuffed in plastic bags and very mouldy.

Now, everyone's focus turned to the upcoming Rugby World Cup. The Springboks were coming to Wellington and although tickets to the matches were expensive and a student budget doesn't usually stretch that far, missing the games was not an option either. Some Kiwi ingenuity was needed and it did not take long for the boys to devise a plan. They decided the game would be best viewed from a grandstand in the lounge, built around their forty-two-inch television screen. Making enough room for friends was a priority. If they had asked the girls' opinion they may have hesitated, so the boys seized the moment and just did it. Chrisjan coordinated the effort with enthusiasm.

The day before the Rugby World Cup began, Jono took a day off university and together they worked like a well-oiled machine.

He remembers the action. "Chrisjan got his band of merry men together including Simo and a guy called Dave Ayling, who is a legend. We went round to all these different places to get crates, loaded them all onto a trailer, and brought them back to the flat. It took a few trips. Then we went and grabbed a whole lot of old couches from any person we could find. Then we started constructing this grandstand."

An hour or two later the boys had rigged up three stands, like an amphitheatre, all facing the large television screen. The boys felt that the grandstand was the greatest achievement of their lives. They thought that the top tier would hold four people safely. In fact, twelve people sat on it and nothing broke. On the first night of the tour, Melvyn counted fifty-six people there.

By the time Lucy, Vicky and the other girls came in, the lounge was in a state of chaotic transformation and they wondered what on earth was happening. "It was massively high," Lucy recalls. "The top tier was right in front of the boys' room, blocking off the door. Chrisjan told me, 'Jump on this couch. Now get on that one. Look! See how stable it is.' He was really proud of his achievement. All the guys were." When Vicky sat on a couch and commented that it was a bit wobbly, Chrisjan told her, "No it's not . . . You should not criticise it."

A couple of days after the grandstand was completed, the landlord happened to call in for a flat inspection. The flatmates were extremely relieved and rather surprised that he did not object. In fact, after his visit they decided more seats were needed. Figuring the space was a bit cramped, they made some improvements, adding on a fourth stand. By this point, the windows were nearly completely boarded up because the couches were right up against the windows. So, they decided to sacrifice the use of their front door and the door to Melvyn and Chrisjan's bedroom, so they could get another stand in. Now there was only a tiny space for Chrisjan and Melvyn to access their room. Melvyn could just slither through. Chrisjan would swing himself in, an audible thump sounding as he hit the ground. It was like that for six weeks.

Alexis would often turn up to watch the games, or the movies afterwards. Finally, the grandstand was taken down, leaving the flatmates amazed at how much floor space they had gained.

~

When Chrisjan went home for Christmas that year, he promised his parents he would return in February with Alexis. He wanted to introduce them to his girlfriend and he wanted her to meet the rest of his family. For now, the photo he gave them would have to do. He was so happy that his parents had been able to re-establish their family home and were both living in one place. After several job changes, Jan had secured a position on a farm close to Heriot which meant Annie could keep her teaching job at the school.

There was almost as much to celebrate as the first time they had been all reunited on the farm at Balfour. In contrast to their first New Zealand Christmas, summer had turned up on cue this year. In fact, temperatures soared on the twenty-fifth of December and, once the eating and the presents were done, they were content to relax and enjoy each other's company. Someone suggested taking photos but it was so hot, everyone was tired, and it never quite happened. It was the last time the Jordaan family were all together.

CHAPTER TWENTY-EIGHT

# WE'RE GOING TO FLY HIGH

The seventh of January was a date Chrisjan really wanted to be a surprise. He asked Alexis to keep the day free, and had simply written in her diary, "We're going to fly high."

Everyone in his flat knew what he had planned but agreed not to tell her. Somehow though, the secret was leaked. When her girlfriends realised, they made a pact not to tell Chrisjan that Alexis knew. But even those intentions came unstuck. Snippets of conversation slipped unnoticed between coffee and takeaways on the couch and eventually he found out. Some of his mates thought the whole idea sounded too serious, almost like a proposal scenario. But Chrisjan was unperturbed. Their adventure was still a few days away, and for now, his focus was on helping to clean out the flat in Tinakori Road. After two years together, the friends were all moving on, heading in different directions.

During the first week in January, the boys stacked up eighteen bags of rubbish that dwarfed the backyard. It was hard work but they got the job done. Early on Friday evening, Alexis came over and helped Chrisjan cook his favourite meatballs for dinner. As always, they went down a treat. But it was the day ahead that was foremost in Chrisjan's mind. He had received a text from a balloon company in Carterton, a small town not too far from the nation's capital, advising conditions were expected to be perfect for a flight the following morning. Hot air balloon flights are weather dependent, and the booking had already been postponed twice. At last, it looked like it was actually going to happen and Chrisjan was stoked. Hot air ballooning certainly had the wow factor, and he hoped it would take their nearly-year-old relationship to a whole new level. "Just pray that we get up tomorrow," Chrisjan said to his friends later that night.

At that moment, none of them could have imagined the tragedy that was about to unfold.

~

Clayton and Leanne Brown were quite used to seeing hot air balloons overhead. Sometimes they even landed on their property, a small holding where they farmed a pig stud called Wallowing Heights. The couple were early risers; that day they were up before six o'clock in the morning because Clayton was heading out to the coast to do some fishing. Leanne was keen to go with him at first but then decided against it. For some unexplained reason, she felt that she should stay home and do some jobs. When he drove off, she was still in her dressing gown, relaxing on their veranda, enjoying the stillness of the warm, hazy morning.

When Leanne looked up and saw a balloon approaching overhead, an uncanny feeling came over here, as if there was something amiss. A momentary fear that the balloon might crash flickered through her mind. Grabbing her gumboots, she pulled them on and hurried round the back of the house, visually tracking the flight path. As she stood there watching it hover, she could see the passengers above waving, chatting and laughing. Everything appeared quite normal. And yet, Leanne's ominous foreboding feeling became stronger. As the balloon drifted beyond the property and looked as if it might land without incident, she figured she was just being paranoid. Yet it seemed as if a magnet kept drawing her gaze back towards it.

Leanne noticed the balloon was heading her way again. She decided she should get dressed but only reached the kitchen when she heard a thunderous *bang*. Pulling on her gumboots once again, she dashed outside, only to see the basket snared in power lines, right on the boundary of their property, just behind the house. The men and the pilot onboard were trying to lift the wires to free the basket. Seeing the situation, Leanne's mind went into overdrive, scrambling to think what resources she might have that would be of assistance.

Suddenly, the balloon lurched upwards again, but it was still caught by the power lines. A small fire had appeared at the base of the basket. Leanne heard the urgency in the voices of the men, giving instructions to each other, as they worked to free the trapped balloon. It seemed they were unaware of the fire, and, yelling to alert them, she called 111 emergency services from her mobile, never taking her eyes off the unfolding drama. It was 7:22 a.m. The call was one minute and eight seconds long, with Leanne willing her voice to give clear, concise details. She told the operator she was fully expecting passengers to begin jumping at any moment and was poised to act.

Alexis was the first to jump. Leanne looked up to see Chrisjan urging and assisting her to get up and out of the basket. In that instant, she saw his selfless, caring character. Moments later, Chrisjan followed her. As they cartwheeled earthwards, the power lines above them broke and the fire in the basket took hold.

Leanne had no formal first aid training but after raising four children in the country she had learnt a thing or two. She ran towards the spot where Alexis and Chrisjan had landed, and knelt to feel for a pulse. Then, ensuring each of them was in the recovery position, she began to administer CPR. She somehow knew that these two were a couple, and the way they had fallen only served to confirm her intuition. They were lying in the shape of a cross. Leanne yelled for help, and seconds later, when her son came running out, she urged him to alert the arriving emergency services personnel and direct them to the scene. It was only when Chrisjan and Alexis were in the care of the paramedics that Leanne felt she could leave them. She believed they would survive.

Now she turned her attention to the livestock. Pigs are terrified of electricity and the broken, live lines were lying nearby. Moving as quickly as she could, she shifted the pigs and other stock in anticipation that the gates to her property would need to be opened to give access for ambulances and other emergency vehicles.

Finally, she returned to where Chrisjan and Alexis were lying. She had presumed that the passengers would be taken to the hospital for treatment. Now she was confronted by the reality that both Chrisjan and Alexis had already died. Engulfed in a sense of disbelief, Leanne went back into the house and gathered matching blankets to cover their bodies. They were blankets she had bought many years before, at the time of her son's birth. As a mum, she could not bear to leave someone else's children lying there alone, so she decided to stay beside them, together with the police officer who had been dispatched to the site.

When her husband, Clayton, arrived home sometime later, he could not believe the scene he encountered, either at his own home, or at the neighbouring property where the charred balloon had landed. The tragedy had ripped into their world with cruel disregard for their peaceful, ordered lives.

CHAPTER TWENTY-NINE

# BACK AT THE FLAT

*The darker the night, the brighter the stars, the deeper the grief, the closer is God.*
*Fyodor Dostoyevsky*

When news of the tragedy first began to filter through news bulletins, text messages and social media, time seemed to stand still while Chrisjan and Alexis' friends were catapulted into devastating confusion, shock and denial. Frantic with concern, Alexis' friend and Chrisjan's flatmate, Vicky, called Alexis' parents. Jono tried to call the balloon company. Melvyn called their ARISE youth pastor, Ben Carroll. Others were trying to make contact with Alexis and Chrisjan on their mobile phones. With no confirmation of events, searching for the truth became of utmost importance. Any possibility or logical explanation became a precious shred of hope.

The Tinakori flatmates hoped Chrisjan and Alexis' flight was with a different balloon company. They hoped that maybe the car had broken down and their friends hadn't made it to Carterton in time. They tried asking the police for information. No one could concentrate on what they were doing that Saturday morning. Those working in summer jobs asked for leave. Lucy, who was back home in Napier preparing to celebrate her twenty-first birthday, cancelled the party and got on the next flight back to Wellington. Joe was writing his thesis but couldn't focus after hearing the news. Nate and some of the other guys from the life group were helping with a sausage sizzle fundraiser. They excused themselves. Saturday suddenly seemed so surreal, almost as if they were living outside of time.

When Ben Carroll arrived at the flat, he was as much in shock as everyone else. He knew Chrisjan well, but knew that this was no time to dwell on his own feelings and fears. Guessing it was going to be a long day while they waited for updates, he suggested the boys continue with the clean-up they had begun earlier in the week and pitched in to lend a hand. Occupying themselves productively helped them stay positive and hopeful.

While they worked, they waited for news, for confirmation, for any snippet of hope, but details were sketchy. No one knew for sure, but deep down, they had begun to guess that both of their friends were gone. By the end of the day, around seventy people had gathered at the flat in Tinakori Road. Ben remembers, "By the time we came to say grace for dinner, the reality that they had died was beginning to sink in. Because there was no official call from anyone, we didn't know one hundred percent, but we didn't really need that call. I remember saying grace and pretty much cracking under the emotion of it all. It wasn't just a token 'Thank you, Lord, bless this food.' I remember I really felt God's presence and also an overwhelming sense of grief."

After dinner, some of the boys went outside to play cricket or to shoot basketball hoops. The girls were inside. There was a lot of crying but a little laughter too as they recalled stories of Chrisjan's stubbies, his decision to buy skinny jeans, and how he hated it when guys wore pink clothes. Late in the day, they gathered in the courtyard. Someone had brought a guitar. They cried and prayed as they sang a song Ben had written sometime earlier, 'Who is Like You?' It expressed thoughts from Psalm 139 that no matter where we are or how dark the situation, God is still faithful and deserves our praise.

That night some of the girls huddled together in the same bed. Any thoughts of sleep were dissolved in the rain that poured down the whole night. Vicky reflected that it was like "the earth was mourning. It felt like God was crying for his lost children." Jono felt as if the earth was screaming out. "It was like when Jesus died on the cross, there were earthquakes and storms," he said.

It was still raining the next morning when they went to church. Tears flowed almost as freely as the rain outside. The immense grief and numbing shock seemed almost too painful to bear. A visiting pastor from Australia, Graham Kirkwood, was scheduled to speak at ARISE that morning. He had been asked to prepare a sermon on joy. A week beforehand he had forwarded the PowerPoint presentation he had prepared. He knew nothing of the tragedy, yet while flying across the Tasman, he felt strongly that God was impressing on him that he should preach on a text found in Psalm

30:5: "Weeping may last through the night, but joy comes with the morning." To preach on joy in the face of such calamity must have seemed absurd and yet, for a Christian, that verse epitomises hope and provides a grip on life, even in the face of unthinkable catastrophe.

ARISE Church's Senior Pastor, John Cameron, was scheduled to speak in Sydney at Hillsong Church that Sunday, but he flew back as soon as he heard the news. He knew he needed to be with his congregation. He led them as they began to walk through the deep, dark valley of the shadow of death. Reality was hard to accept. Grief was still raw. And yet, the positive qualities of this couple were an inspiration.

That Sunday evening at church, Pastor John highlighted the values by which Chrisjan and Alexis lived. He touched on the many ways these two young people had made a difference in the world. They served where they saw a need, and believed that change was possible. They were inclusive and consistent. They valued the young and honoured the old. They drew their inner strength from God. The positive influence they had in people's lives was a testimony to their character.

Youth pastor, Ben Carroll, focussed his reflections around a verse from Philippians 1:20–21: *"I eagerly expect and hope that I will in no way be ashamed, but will have sufficient courage so that now as always Christ will be exalted in my body, whether by life or by death. For to me, to live is Christ and to die is gain."*

Ben was personally challenged by Chrisjan's courage. A quote from William Wallace in *Braveheart*, one of Chrisjan's favourite movies, seemed to sum up his life: "Men don't follow titles, they follow courage." Ben had watched Chrisjan growing in both courage and leadership. He saw a young man who believed that no sacrifice was too big and acted out his beliefs in spite of criticism. He chose to change his career path because he wanted to work for justice and equality for others. On Sunday mornings, when his sound and lighting pack-in team was rostered on, he did not complain about having a four o'clock in the morning start to the day. When it came to relationship issues, he was not too proud to ask advice from his leaders.

Ben saw courage exemplified in the steps Chrisjan and Alexis took as a couple. He couldn't help but notice the way in which they lived and served, even when no one was looking. Together they valued, honoured and believed in people, even if they got nothing in return. They followed their dreams. They shared their faith without compromise. For these two, it was important to stand up for what was right, even if it was unpopular.

His concluding comments summed up both of their lives: "Courage is actually only revealed in the living of life . . . it is revealed in the choices you make . . . it is formed over a lifetime but only revealed in the moment. For Chrisjan and Alexis, I know they lived courageous lives because of the choices they made to follow God's call despite other options . . . Life is too short to be selfish and live for ourselves. We must choose courage over complacency. We must follow our convictions rather than what is convenient."

For Ben Carroll, these are two people whom he will always remember. In 2015 he reflected, "For the last three years I could honestly say there would not be many days where I haven't thought about Chrisjan and Alexis, not for long periods of time... but they are engraved on our hearts and minds forever. I know it's a bit weird, but I often think of them as angels who came and visited for a short time but will never be forgotten."

CHAPTER THIRTY

# SHOCKWAVES OF GRIEF

*No one ever told me that grief felt so like **fear**.*
*C. S. Lewis*

As news of the tragedy reverberated throughout the country, friends of Chrisjan and Alexis were engulfed with numbing shock and disbelief.

**The Stevenson Family**

On January 7, 2012, Barry and Lynne were, as usual, beginning to think about their annual excursion to Glendhu Bay. Important words like *boat*, *tent*, and *chilly bin* were suddenly replaced with words like *Carterton*, *hot air balloon*, and *tragedy*. Disbelief silenced their conversation.

Sam was in Dunedin, working on his computer. "It wasn't long before we went to Glendhu," he recalls. "A friend posted an article online about what had happened. When I read through it and Chrisjan's name popped up, I sort of froze. I read it three more times to confirm it. I couldn't get over it. It was a freak accident that happened to probably the only friend I had in Wellington. It took a long time to sink in." Sam sent a text to his dad, who could not believe what he was reading and thought it must be a mistake. They all agreed it was the hardest Glendhu summer they had ever had.

"We missed our extra son," Barry reflected. "I don't know what it's like to lose a son, but I do know what it's like to lose a child who is close to you. Chrisjan was one of those. But that's the way it goes; unfortunately, we can't do anything about it. Being a religious boy, it might not have been 'before his time'. Maybe there was something better for him."

Sam was stunned. "If you were going to put it in terms of probability, it's a million to one," he said. "The cancellations they'd had, the number of other people there could have been . . ."

Lynne also pondered the gap he had left. "He was with us for such a short time, yet he impacted our lives so much. He wanted to improve so many people's lives; that was what he wanted to do."

**The African Team**

*Linda Cousins* wrote, "The night that we found out, I really struggled. My big thing was saying to God, 'You said that if we cry out to you that you would send your angels to protect us.' I knew that they would have cried out, and I really struggled with that . . . I think it helped me a lot just knowing they were together, that they loved God, and that I know where they are. There is no shadow of doubt that they are in heaven together, and right up until that last minute, Chrisjan put Alexis first. He was true to her, right to the last second."

*Susan Guyton* recalls, "I was really excited that Saturday. We were to have the first prayer meeting for the New Year at my house. Chrisjan had organised it. He wanted us to pray specifically for Africa and to inspire others with the vision of outreach. Justin called me in the morning. He was crying and I couldn't hear exactly what he was saying. I didn't believe him . . . I was thinking they would walk through the door soon, there must be a mistake. I continued to prepare for the *braai*, or barbeque, praying I would hear a knock at the door . . . Pastor Ben Carroll rang me and said we should move the braai to Chrisjan's flat where others could join us. I think by four o'clock, we knew. But you just go numb, and you don't believe it has happened, and then the reality of it hits you. But spiritually you get kind of angry and you start thinking, *God what is going on? Why them? Would it have been better if it was me?* They had so much to live for; they were so committed, and they had so much in the future dedicated to God, lives surrendered to His calling."

She recalls the months following the accident: "I had this period of time when I didn't want to be with anyone. I just wanted to be at home and sleep all the time. People would say, 'You just have to hang out.' I struggled to sleep at night and then I would sleep the whole day. That probably went on for three or four months until eventually I snapped out of it . . . Then five months later, in May, my younger brother passed away, and you think, *Oh, my gosh. What is going on?* Spiritually, I was challenged quite a lot. As a Christian, you know that God is in the centre of it all, but these kinds of things are just too hard. But when you rise out of it, you always rise up stronger and fired up for God, to do whatever He wants with your life. Chrisjan was like one of God's generals. I feel so inspired to pick up the mantle, to run with the baton that has been handed on, to see lives changed and God's name glorified. I had prayed with him and, when Chrisjan prayed, he prayed the roof down. He could pray for ten minutes or more, even in a prayer meeting that lasted for only half an hour. So, you heard his heart, his dreams and his vision and you also heard God."

*Justin Grobler* said, "For me personally, the thing that challenged me through this was what people remembered about Chrisjan. What will people remember about me? No one is going to talk about my possessions or intentions—no one cares about them—people remember actions. Chrisjan inspired me to value relationships more. He inspired me to never give up on somebody even if they are running away from me. He taught me that if there is someone in my life who is going through a struggle, that I shouldn't be afraid to reach out into that situation and try to help that person through it. He would have done that. It's about realigning your life-long goals. I can spend my whole life working for money or I can spend my whole life reaching out to people and in the end, it is going to be the people story not the money story that is remembered.

*Noel McCardle* reflects, "For me, 2012 was a difficult year with the accident as well as the passing of my father-in-law and my brother. However, the inspiration of having known Chrisjan, and his faith, helped me come through the year stronger in my walk with God. God turns all things for good, even though you ask, 'Why?'"

## Friends from Gore

On 7 January 2012, Sam Johnstone was up in Central Otago, spending a few days of the summer holidays with friends. They had been in full party-mode, celebrating the New Year, yet it had left Sam feeling somewhat unfulfilled. A few days later he was driving around with his mates in the car when a text message came through to his mobile. He pulled over to read it, and suddenly, his life, which seemed so together on the outside, felt wrecked from the inside out.

That night he prayed, for the first time in a long time, and reconnected with God. Later he commented, "Really good people die every day. You can question it, but we can't really understand why these things happen. Tragic as it was, it hasn't really angered me; it's a broken world. I think God is going to use it somehow to do some good. I kept a couple of his funeral pamphlets and put them in whatever room I am staying in at the time. I see Chrisjan's picture every day and think about the feeling I had when I realised I would never see him again. I just try to honour his life with mine as much as I can. I miss him."

James Bruce writes, "I went to Chrisjan's funeral and saw all these people he has impacted, and I came away saying, 'God why? Why did you do that?' I searched for a little bit, for a lot, and I'm still sort of searching, I suppose. But one verse that I've come to is this: 'The rain will fall on the righteous and the unrighteous and the sun will shine on the just and the unjust (Matthew 5:45). We are in a fallen world. Crap happens and God is good. God is big . . . but I continually ask God, 'Why him? Why couldn't you take me?' But in a way that's selfish. Chrisjan was at that place where he truly relied on God and was like 'No sacrifice is too great.' God didn't make that hot air balloon situation happen. God didn't do that to him. It wasn't God. We live in a fallen world and things happen. People die. I'm starting to realise it's not God's fault."

**Alexis' Friends**

At Alexis' funeral, one of her closest friends, Eliana, sang a song she had written as a personal poignant tribute. It was a hard call but she knew that if Alexis had been sitting there when she stood with her guitar to sing, she would have encouraged her to be strong. Some weeks later, Eliana went shopping with three of Alexis' friends from Hawkes Bay—Krista, Julia and Rachel. They each bought a matching plain sterling silver ring and had them engraved with a quote Alexis had written on the wall in her room: *Praat vir ander,* which is Afrikaans for 'Speak up for others.' Wearing the rings has continued to deeply impact their individual lives and continues to be an inspiration and a symbol of strength for each of them to fulfil their dreams, push boundaries and make a difference in the world by helping others.

**Massey University**

Early in 2013, Massey University awarded posthumous degrees to both Chrisjan and Alexis. Anmari received Chrisjan's certificate, while Alexis' siblings, Emma and Ben, accepted hers. There was a standing ovation. After the ceremony, Annie and Anmari were overwhelmed when the life group boys gave them a Springbok rugby jersey with "No. 2 Jordaan" on the back. It was a special tribute, covered with signed messages:

> CJ, my dear friend – Gonna miss you like crazy. Who's going to telepath with me now? Closer than a brother. You are a true champion. Miss you, bro —Jono

> My friend, you will be missed. Seeing you later, bro —Simon

> CJ, the legend. I am missing you man but I know I'll be reunited again. Love you man. You've left a massive legacy —Simo

> Bro, thank you for making me the man I am today. Miss you and love you.

> Inspiration. Miss you, bro —Nate

> CJ, your love, support and encouragement saved my life —Tom

> So glad to have met you. See you soon —Justin

> True man of God. Love you, CJ.

> You will always be in our heart, bro —Zac

> Thank you, legend —JW

> Hey roomie. I miss you man. See you soon —Melvyn

> It's been an honour and a blessing to know you. I'll miss you, hehe.

Hey CJ, all I can say is thanks for letting us clean your front yard. Miss you so much.

Hey bro, I have always looked up to you and bro, I will never stop —James

Chrisjan, there are no words. We will never forget you. You taught us so much. Miss you, bro —Jimmy

Chrisjan, you inspire me. You're an awesome guy —Vicky

Death may have taken you but the grave doesn't hold. No sacrifice is too big. You're an inspiration —Joey

**World Vision**

Chrisjan and Alexis are remembered by World Vision not only in New Zealand but also in Africa. During the months following the tragedy, two of their friends, Evelyn and Britney, began a fundraising project to honour their memory. Evelyn was one of the team members who went to Africa. They chose to support the Sindeya village school in the central Malawian district of Dowa, one of seven schools providing education for children from two hundred and twenty-three villages. At the time, nine teachers were struggling to teach seven hundred and twenty-three students in just four classrooms. The toilet block was primitive and woefully inadequate. Both girls were keen to promote this worthwhile cause. A poignant poem by Nan Witcomb was included in the brochure seeking support for the Sindeya project:

*To mourn too long*
*for those we love*
*is self-indulgent –*
*but to honour the memory*
*with a promise*
*to live a little better*
*for having known them,*
*gives purpose to their life –*
*and some reason*
*for their death . . .*

At the ARISE women's conference that year, an offering was taken for the school. Those funds were further boosted by the proceeds from a drama show, performed and planned by the children who Alexis had taught. To complete the project, Chrisjan's parents donated the money they had given him on his twenty-first birthday. After the accident it was still sitting in his savings account. They believed it was only appropriate to donate the money for the Sindeya project.

As a result, the Sindeya School now has two extra classrooms and a new toilet block. One hundred and twenty school desks were purchased. School enrolment has nearly doubled, and school absenteeism has reduced. The children are more motivated to go to school because there is an improved learning environment with desks, textbooks and sporting equipment all available. On every child's desk in the junior block at the school there is a small plaque in memory of Chrisjan and Alexis. They would have been astonished.

## Chrisjan's Parents

For the Jordaan family, the years since the accident have tested them deeply. Grief has many faces and everyone copes in different ways. Coming to terms with losing someone you love is difficult, but when that person is in the prime of life, and when everything they stand for is good, their death is a cruel blow. At first, joy was hard to find for Jan and Annie Jordaan. But as the years have passed, they have come to realise that though they struggle to accept their loss, the past cannot be changed and they must move on.

Annie's heart often aches, especially on Chrisjan's birthday and at Christmas. She recalls the promise she made to God that her son would belong to Him forever. She believes there was a greater purpose for his life. She also wonders if God, who sees the big picture, knew that coping with hard times in the future would have been too difficult for Chrisjan. Her thoughts are echoed in the Bible: "Good people pass away; the godly often die before their time . . . no one seems to understand that God is protecting them from the evil to come" (Isaiah 57:1).

Jan coped in a different way. Shortly after the tragedy he was walking past the cenotaph in Gore. Pausing to consider the lists of names of more than one hundred and fifty men from the district who died in the two great wars, he guessed that some of them, like Chrisjan, would have been twenty-one years of age. The inscription from 1 Corinthians 15:54-55, etched on the front of the cenotaph captured his attention: "Death is swallowed up in victory." It was almost like an epiphany. The quote was familiar—he recognised it from the Bible—and the truth of the words resonated deeply in his spirit, as if they had been written just for him.

From that moment he knew, without any doubt, that Chrisjan was safe. His faith was in a God who promised victory even in the face of tragedy and death. For him it was like ballast, a counterweight, a stabiliser that helps to keep a person upright in the face of unimaginable heartache.

At his son's memorial service marking the first anniversary of the accident, Jan thanked ARISE church for their part in Chrisjan's life. "He came to Wellington as a young boy and became a man here, with a purpose in life and something to work towards . . . The past cannot be changed. But we can change tomorrow. We can't bring Chrisjan and Alexis back, but what they stood for can go on." He finished by issuing a challenge to move on and to honour the memory of Chrisjan and Alexis in the most effective way possible by continuing their legacy.

# COMMEMORATIONS

Chrisjan filled every moment of his life with purpose and intention. Each morning in the Tinakori Road flat he woke to words of inspiration, handwritten on pieces of paper, covering his bedroom walls. He could not have known that two of them were almost prophetic. The first quote was written in capital letters: NO SACRIFICE IS TOO BIG. Chrisjan lived his life for others because he believed that every person has a purpose. He believed he was doing what God asked him to do. He believed in changing the world one person at a time.

The other quote touched his family deeply and they had the words engraved on his headstone in the small, peaceful Crookston cemetery in West Otago, where his ashes have been interred.

*Even when we pass away, God still answers our prayers.*

~

In Somerset Road, about two hundred metres apart, the tragedy was commemorated in two very different ways. Clayton and Leanne Brown transformed their property, Wallowing Heights, into an interactive family farm park that was officially opened in December 2012. It was like a touchstone for grieving families, for the local community, and for many other people. The sign at the entrance said it all:

*This area is dedicated to Chrisjan Jordaan and Alexis Still.*

*Live, Laugh, Play.*

Children and their families went for birthday parties or for a treat. They had fun in the playhouse, on the little bridge, or on the swing. They looked for rabbits among the flowerpots, or discovered little treasures hidden on the tree. Everything was painted in red or yellow—favourite colours of Chrisjan and Alexis. Away from the public eye, a small enclosure bordered by a yellow fence marked the spot where Chrisjan and Alexis jumped. It provided a private, almost sacred place of remembrance for the Still and Jordaan families. Their parents planted a golden tree there as a living memorial to their children. The other nine victims of the tragedy were not forgotten either. Clayton and Leanne planted nine fruit trees, each in a colourful plastic tub, where the respective families wrote messages. Sadly, due to ill health, the park was closed in December 2016 and the property has since been sold.

~

On a neighboring property nearer the main road, two trees mark the final resting place of the balloon carrying the remaining nine passengers. For four years, nothing else identified the spot. But in 2015, in response to a letter from family members and requests from the Carterton community, the Carterton District Council agreed that it was both appropriate and timely to erect a public memorial. The landowner, Graeme Tulloch, generously donated a small area of his property at the roadside edge to be used; it is screened by a wooden fence to create a personal space. A wooden seat, built by the local Rotary Club, gives people the opportunity to sit and reflect. Eleven names are etched on a granite plaque, set in a limestone rock which was sourced in the area. Each name represents a person who had a story, a family, hopes and dreams, all of which remain engraved in the hearts and minds of those who were closest to them.

A beautiful unveiling service was held on January 7, 2016, the fourth anniversary of the accident. It was one of those moments when time stands still and you hardly dare to breathe. Unspoken memories silently linked parents, siblings, family members, friends, service personnel, Somerset Road residents, and people from the local community who gathered for the ceremony. Even the blustery wind seemed to quieten down as the service began. Every contribution was moving and meaningful, beginning with a karanga. The words of the reading "They Are Gone," followed by Andy Eldred's poem "What is Life?" and his song, "Carrying You, Carrying Me" all acknowledged the sadness of loss, yet spoke of hope, love and grace, all of which give strength and resilience to face the future.

Before unveiling the memorial, the then mayor, John Booth, briefly addressed those gathered, expressing the community's care and support for the families and all those so deeply affected by the tragedy. He expressed hope that the site would now be a place of reflection, and a help in the healing process. The names of the victims were read and a minute's silence was observed. A small flock of pigeons was released and disappeared swiftly into the heavens, signifying peace, hope, and new beginnings. As the formalities drew to a close, strains of a *waiata* (Maori song) softly permeated the air. Along the road at Wallowing Heights, the leaves on the golden tree shimmered and danced in the sunlight. In the space of the few short years gifted to them, Chrisjan and Alexis had truly celebrated life in all its fullness, and now together, with their hands firmly in the hand of their God, they had danced into eternity.

# WHAT IS LIFE?

*Is life a journey or a dream or a thought?*
*Is life joy and laughter; is it things we have bought?*
*Is life adventure, and the chances we take?*
*Is life a career and the things that we make?*
*Is life a risk, a dangerous dare?*
*Is life being angry and a time of despair?*
*Is life simply seconds and hours and days?*
*Is life the childlike games that we play?*
*Is life watching sunsets on romantic dates?*
*Is life watching children discover their fates?*
*Is life a sensation and meals that we share?*
*Is life all we love and all those who care?*
*Is life doing things that we dream we can do?*
*Is life flying high in a hot air balloon?*
*Is life a time of suffering, a time of grief and pain?*
*Is life little children dancing in the summer rain?*
*Is life standing in a sacred place remembering all that's past?*
*Is life holding precious moments that we know can never last?*
*Is life just a moment, a moment that is blessed?*
*To those who have truly lived life, the answer to all is yes!*

*by Rev Andy Eldred*

*The 'grandstand' at the flat in Tinokori, Wellington. Chrisjan is in the centre.*

*Christjan loved to cook up a feast (or 'braai') on the barbeque*

*Helping out on the Lipiri Development Project in Malawi*

*Chrisjan hanging out with African children as part of the World Vision trip trip to Malawi with ARISE Church*

*Christjan and Alexis at his 21st birthday*

*Christmas 2010 Jordaan family photo*
*From left—Anmari, Jan, Chrisjan, Annie, Elrie*

*Chrisjan and Alexis with the balloon before the launch (Photo credit: Geoff Walker)*

*A lasting monument to those killed in the Carterton balloon tragedy*

# ABOUT THE AUTHOR

VALMAI REDHEAD is an emerging author who grew up in Dunedin but has spent most of her adult life in Gore. She believes that writing stories matters. Her library career nurtured a passion for books about people who have made a difference. When first asked to write this story, she felt daunted by the challenge. Yet as his family and close friends shared their memories with raw honesty, a consistent thread emerged of Chrisjan's strong character underpinned by a deep Christian faith. He was a young man whose life touched and influenced many people in countless positive ways. Birthing this story was a labour of love fraught with many unexpected detours en route. But what a thrill to see it finally completed and published. His parents' wish is that his story will inspire others and in some way continue his legacy of making a difference in the world, one person at a time. May their prayer be answered.

www.ingramcontent.com/pod-product-compliance
Lightning Source LLC
Chambersburg PA
CBHW031251290426
44109CB00012B/527